Singing and the Imagination of Devotion

Vocal Aesthetics in Early English Protestant Culture

Susan Tara Brown

WIPF & STOCK · Eugene, Oregon

Wipf and Stock Publishers
199 W 8th Ave, Suite 3
Eugene, OR 97401

Singing and the Imagination of Devotion
Vocal Aesthetics in Early English Protestant Culture
By Brown, Susan Tara
Copyright©2008 Paternoster
ISBN 13: 978-1-60608-314-7
Publication date 1/24/2011
Previously published by Paternoster, 2008

This Edition published by Wipf and Stock Publishers
by arrangement with Paternoster

Contents

Acknowledgements

In chronological order, my gratitude first goes to the clergymen and divines in the seventeenth century who put their (always varied and often fascinating) thoughts concerning singing and the devotional life down on paper—thoughts upon which, over three hundred years later, this study is based. I hope they would not be displeased with the product! More recent in time, I wish to thank the helpful staffs at the Beinecke Rare Book and Manuscript Library at Yale University, the William Andrews Clark Memorial Library at the University of California in Los Angeles, and the Huntington Library. Financial support for my post-doctoral research came from the Association for Religion in Intellectual Life, the UCLA Center for Seventeenth and Eighteenth-Century Studies, and the Huntington Library. I am also indebted to those who have read and made helpful suggestions on the manuscript, including Dale Bruner, Steven Guthrie, Michael Horton, Paul Howden, and James Packer. Jeremy Mudditt, Robin Parry, and the rest of the staff at Paternoster have been a delight to work with. Vicki Finklestein has been a tremendous help with her computing and secretarial expertise. Finally, I wish to thank those closest to me—my family—for their ever-present love and support.

'A Paul and Silas, turn a Dungeon into a Palace, by Singing there. One says, The Earth Danced unto their Music.'
— *The Accomplished Singer*

Introduction

In more sentimental books on music from the past, one sometimes encounters the romantic claim that a certain era or people 'loved to sing,' 'filled their waking hours with song,' 'had melody in their souls,' and so on. The modern musicologist or ethnomusicologist ardently avoids writing anything redolent of such happy platitudes. But perhaps our predecessors were onto something. For the more we explore early modern English thought, the more it appears to indicate a society intrigued by singing to a remarkable degree, both in theory and in practice. Singing played a vital role in England's devotional life during this era; and it would not be too much to assert that the nation's devotional life, in turn, ultimately affected its social, moral, and political spheres as well.

This is a study in vocal aesthetics derived from early English Protestant theological writings: a type of intellectual and social history, or meta-analysis, of the practice of singing itself. Its sources carry the scent of a dynamic age marked by political upheaval, religious controversy, and cultural change. England during this period is often regarded as a musicological backwater, and most people have but a vague idea of that country's musical life in the murky years between Dowland and Purcell. It would seem that artistic energies were otherwise occupied in an era of civil war and endless power struggles. Despite this seemingly fallow ground, however, the idea for this study came from my own research in seventeenth-century English devotional song, a rich, albeit neglected, genre, which ranges in complexity from simple psalter melodies to elaborate mini-dramas featuring the metaphysical conceits of George Herbert and John Donne.[1] We might already guess that singing played a prominent role in congregational worship; but it took place in private and household devotions as well; and the many psalters and devotional song collections printed during this era only confirm our sense of its ubiquity. Following the lead of Paul in Eph. 5:18-19: 'Be filled with the Spirit, speaking to one another in psalms and hymns and spiritual songs, singing and making melody with your heart to the Lord,' musical settings of the Psalms, hymns, and para-liturgical devotional songs were sung by all

---

1 The most comprehensive studies of this genre are Ronald Anderson's 'Richard Alison's Psalter (1599) and Devotional Music in England to 1640' (Ph.D. diss., University of Iowa, 1974); and Susan Treacy's 'English Devotional Song of the Seventeenth-Century in Printed Collections from 1638 to 1693: A Study of Music and Culture' (Ph. D. diss., North Texas State University, 1986).

classes of English society, in public and at home; and numerous biographies of Anglicans and Puritans alike attest to the fact that singing was valued and cultivated as a means of private devotional expression. The human voice consequently took on many practical and symbolic functions, such as mirror of the soul, conduit to the heart, and template of the affections.

Studying English devotional song eventually led me to the Protestant devotional writers who flourished during this period.[2] Although they are an obscure and unexpected source for aesthetic theory, thinkers such as Richard Sibbes, Joseph Hall, William Fenner, and Richard Baxter were fascinated with questions of truth and beauty, the inner landscape, and 'heavenly-mindedness'; and their writings present a unified and comprehensive opinion on the value of singing; the unique nature of the human voice; desired conditions of mind during 'performance'; and the personal changes wrought by singing. Their works were widely dispersed and eagerly received by a reading public, and their philosophies consequently had great influence upon the English Protestant interest in vocal music.

All of this ultimately begs the question to what extent, if any, this period's distinctive aesthetic shapes modern assumptions about singing. This is a question well worth asking, for the subject of singing as a verb is rarely a focus of discussion.[3] While studies on the relationships between music and language abound,[4] largely absent in the literature is any treatment of such basic questions as, is the human voice special or unique as a musical instrument? What have different historic eras and cultures believed about the singing voice as a force in itself? Is there a current teleology, or aesthetic goal, of singing? If so, what is it?[5] While this book will not address all of these issues as they pertain to modern practice, I do

---

2   As well as other figures who wrote on the subject of sacred music, such as John Playford.

3   Omitting the field of performance practice.

4   Don Harran's *Word-Tone Relations in Musical Thought: From Antiquity to the Seventeenth Century* (Stuttgart: American Institute of Musicology, Hanssler-Verlag, 1986) comes to mind (although Harran himself admits that it is not concerned with the 'purely vocal and histrionic aspects of performance'); also John Hollander's *The Untuning of the Sky: Ideas of Music in English Poetry 1500-1700* (Princeton: Princeton University Press, 1961); Elisa Bickford Jorgens's *The Well-Tun'd Word: Musical Interpretations of English Poetry 1597-1651* (Minneapolis: University of Minnesota Press, 1982); Wilfrid Meller's *Harmonious Meeting: a Study of the Relationship between English Music, Poetry and Theatre, c. 1600-1670* (London: Dennis Dobson, 1965); and the work of Louise Schleiner, among others.

5   One recent book does take a new approach towards the subject: John Potter's *Vocal Authority: Singing Style and Ideology* (Cambridge: Cambridge University Press, 1998).

believe that it speaks to deep-seated attitudes toward the human voice which are still present in contemporary culture. The staying power of these ideas is in part due to their chronology, as the period 1575-1710 represents a seminal epoch for both English and colonial American societies. Most major Protestant denominations, for example, had roots in this era, and virtually all contemporary theological arguments are mirrored in seventeenth-century controversies. During this period, as well, England and her colonies were establishing long-standing precedents in the fields of law, government, and politics. In the musical world, the public concert system saw its beginnings during this time; instructional manuals teaching rudiments of theory and instrumental technique represented a booming business for publishers, thus signalling a new, democratic approach to pedagogy; and musical notation was becoming standardized across Europe. The English devotional singing tradition fostered the hymn-writing movement of Isaac Watts and Charles Wesley in the eighteenth century, and primed the popular reception of Handel's sacred oratorios in Augustan-era London. Perhaps most importantly, this tradition contributed towards a quasi-sacred esteem for singing and performers which was further aided by the activity of Handel societies around the world, and which continues strong today, *viz.* the common practice of audiences standing in reverence whenever the 'Hallelujah Chorus' is performed, even in secular halls. I believe that these English Protestant divines, with their penchant for theological precision and their interest in the religious imagination, performed a valuable service by clearly articulating ideas about the meaning and value of singing which many thoughtful people vaguely sense, but have not found hitherto expressed.

I am mindful of the considerable scholarship which goes before me concerning the ancient Platonic and Pythagorean concepts of celestial harmony and music's power over the human spirit.[6] This study differs inasmuch as it focuses specifically upon early English Protestant views of the singing voice. The subject lies within familiar territory, for a century before these divines flourished, Europe's learned musical culture had been fascinated by the capacity of vocal music to raise the affections. Renaissance humanism, with its renewed interest in Quintilian and the founding of the Florentine Camerata, bequeathed a strong interest in ideas concerning the effect of language upon the passions, and the rhetorical tradition represented the primary lens through which this process was

---

6 See Gretchen Finney, 'Ecstasy and Music in Seventeenth-Century England,' *Journal of the History of Ideas* 8 (April 1947); ' "Organical Musick" and Ecstasy,' *Journal of the History of Ideas* 8 (June 1947); and *Musical Backgrounds for English Literature: 1580-1650* (New Brunswick: Rutgers University Press, n.d.).

understood.[7] However, accepting rhetoric's contribution to seventeenth-century ideals of vocal expressivity as a given, this book will investigate a parallel, yet independent strain of thought which arose in England from entirely different sources: theological and spiritual ones. Again, while most of the divines quoted in this book were educated in rhetorical theory (and one could argue that virtually all literature can be reduced to the level of rhetorical structure), the content expressed underneath the tools of technique deserves scholarly consideration as well. For what rhetoric ultimately represented to the seventeenth-century mind was a vehicle for expression: no more and no less.[8]

So while the concept that singing raises the affections was not unique to early modern England, I do believe that a special regard for the human voice grew and flourished as an auxiliary of early English Protestantism, with its well-developed literary tradition, its respect for the revelatory Word, its cultivation of the arts of the mind, and its consuming search for personal integrity in religious expression. If an era can by typified by a universal quest, then the seventeenth century in England was an age obsessed with the Holy Grail of 'heart-sincerity' for, 'out of the heart the tongue speaketh.' Such aspects of the devotional culture formed an ideological context which surrounded the performance and reception of vocal music wherever it occurred, and which was discerned (in varying degrees) according to the erudition and/or spiritual interest of singer and audience. The sources cited in this book originate in the late sixteenth century and continue on into the seventeenth and early eighteenth centuries, an age when Reformation ideals flourished and were widely dispersed in printed form throughout England.[9] English literacy rates increased in large part due to the Protestant enthusiasm for Bible reading.

If this era's factious theological controversies seem endless, they also elucidated an aesthetic of singing as rich as anything western music had yet seen. Like everything else in public worship, singing became a source of

---

7 As singing concerns the intersection of word and text, any study of the subject should assume rhetoric's influence upon the expressive arts of poetry, oratory, and music. Early music specialists today consider knowledge of this musical-rhetorical tradition vital for an accurate interpretation of period song. See Harran, *Word-Tone Relations in Musical Thought*, and Robert Toft's *Tune Thy Musicke to Thy Hart: The Art of Eloquent Singing in England 1597-1622* (Toronto: University of Toronto Press, 1993).

8 'In an age which has come to value interdisciplinary study we can see that rhetoric remains the most natural, perhaps the fundamental tool, for understanding the expression of feeling in artistic form.' Brian Vickers, *In Defence of Rhetoric* (Oxford: Clarendon Press, 1988), 374.

9 Later eighteenth-century Methodism notwithstanding: the Wesleyan revival was exactly that: a *revival* of religious attitudes perceived to have been in decline for decades.

controversy to the type of Protestant mind which relished theological exactitude. As one Nonconformist minister himself complained in the early eighteenth century:

> T'were pity to interrupt the Harmony of our Discourses with the ungrateful Jarrings and Discords of Controversy (the most unsuitable thing in the World to our Present Subject) did not the Difficulties and Scruples of some People require it.[10]

Some of this ground had already been traversed by patristic thinkers; other ideas were developments of a religious revolution which focused on the individual and the inner life; still others came in response to practical situations concerning the use of music in corporate worship. In any case, a number of 'precisianist' questions subsequently arose such as, Does the clergy sing alone, or does the congregation join in? Are professional choristers allowed? Is it right for me to sing a Psalm if I cannot personally identify with it—would that make me a religious hypocrite? Does vocal harmony distract too much from the meaning of the words? Should women join in congregational singing? What about instruments in church? Can we sing hymns, or only Psalms? Or, should we even sing at all during worship—perhaps singing was a supernatural gift which, like tongues, disappeared in the apostolic age? Anglican and Puritan divines responded to this barrage of questions with titles like *Singing of the Psalms a Gospel-Ordinance*, *Singing of Psalms the Duty of Christians*, and *The Accomplished Singer*. Until now, this extensive body of literature has been ignored by musicologists, perhaps because it seems too 'churchy,' the product of a generation of sanctimonious cranks. However, these works perform a valuable function as they draw attention to the deeper meanings of an activity which even professional musicians are liable to take for granted. Early modern England was truly a 'vocally-conscious' era, and has bequeathed to us a body of texts concerning the aesthetic motivations of singing which remains unparalleled in breadth.

Finally, a word should be said about my intentional mixing of Puritan (dissenter, nonconformist) and Anglican sources throughout this book: a step which might seem, at best, uninformed and naïve, and at worst, indicative of a serious misunderstanding of English ecclesiastical and social history.[11] It is beyond my scope to replicate in detail the long and

---

10 Thomas Reynolds, 'Objections considered against the Duty of Singing,' in *Practical Discourses of Singing in the Worship of God, by Several Ministers* (London, 1708), 100.

11 Some may wonder why more English Catholic writers are not included in this study. With the exception of Thomas Wright's *The Passions of the Mind in General* (London, 1604), I found Anglican and Puritan sources to be the most useful for my purposes. The sources were self-selecting. Although some prominent musicians during this period *were* Catholic at various times in their lives (Byrd, Dowland,

complicated chronology of these two different, yet intertwining, factions; indeed, scholars of the period disagree among themselves on this subject. I have found the opinion of Charles and Katherine George, in their book *The English Protestant Mind,* to be most helpful in discerning a fundamental unity in the theology of most Puritan and Anglican writers.[12] Various factors indicate that the boundaries between Protestant religious identities in early modern England were quite fluid, and that Anglican and Puritan/dissenting cultures co-existed and even borrowed freely from each other (even when nonconformity was officially illegal from 1662 to 1689). The royalist poet Francis Quarles, for example, wrote the dedication for Richard Sibbes' Puritan devotional classic *The Soules Conflict with it Selfe.* Charles II made conciliatory overtures to Presbyterians and Independents upon his ascension to the throne, and offered bishoprics to some prominent divines from the Puritan side of the spectrum. Latitudinarian leaders winked approvingly when nonconformists participated in Church of England services through the practice of 'occasional conformity.' Furthermore, while the number of official nonconformists in the period between 1660-1732 has been estimated to have been only five to six percent of the English population, works by Nonconformist authors accounted for *forty* percent of the religious best-sellers of the time.[13] Even allowing for such factors as a higher literacy rate amongst nonconformists (estimated to have comprised 13-15 percent of the literate population in England[14]) and their need for published material in lieu of legalized worship, these numbers suggest that a good number of conformists within the Church of England retained some of their older Calvinist sympathies. Finally, there is the interesting revival of popularity of George Herbert's poetry among late-century dissenters when a metrical version of *The Temple* was published. It seems wisest to conclude, then, that although these two groups (at times) lived and operated in vastly different social circles—one need only compare, for example, the situation of Joseph Hall, at the opulent Carolinian court, with that of John Bunyan, in a cold and damp Bedford jail—their most compelling points of

---

Locke), recusants remained a marginalized segment of English society, and consequently any Roman Catholic influence upon the devotional vocal culture described in these pages was of less import in England than the experience of Protestantism.

12 Although the term 'Anglican' is anachronistic for this period, I use it to distinguish establishment Protestants (those content with the Church of England system) from their Puritan counterparts.

13 N.H. Keeble, *The Literary Culture of Nonconformity in Later Seventeenth-Century England* (Athens: University of Georgia Press, 1987), 136; and C. John Sommerville, *Popular Religion in Restoration England* (Gainesville: University of Florida Press, 1977), 31.

14 Keeble, *Literary Culture,* 136.

disagreement lay in their ecclesiastical and political allegiances, not in matters of basic Christian doctrine.[15] Most of these Protestant writers were educated in the classical philosophers, early church fathers, and Reformation theologians; and as such, they participated in a highly literate culture which valued learning and scholarship. They knew their biblical theology and developed a literary mode of expression characterized by biblical concepts and commonplaces. Barbara Kiefer Lewalski's classic *Protestant Poetics and the Seventeenth-Century Religious Lyric* has shown how this mode influenced such poets as the English metaphysicals John Donne and Herbert; she also recognizes an essential theological unity in early English Protestant writers.[16] Most importantly, it will be seen that these two religious parties concur in their estimation of the value of singing, and the profound role it plays in the cultivation of the inner life.[17]

---

15 Horton Davies notes 'the difference between non-high-church Anglican spirituality and Puritan devotions is negligible.' *Worship and Theology in England: From Andrewes to Baxter and Fox, 1603-1690* (Princeton: Princeton University Press, 1975), 118. Perry Miller writes: 'Puritan thinking was fundamentally so much a repetition of Luther and Calvin, and Puritans were so far from contributing any new ideas, that there is reason to doubt whether a distinctly Puritan thought exists.' *The New England Mind: The Seventeenth Century* (Cambridge: Harvard University Press, 1954), 92. It is apparent that Laudian Anglicanism differed significantly, both in theology and in spiritual attitudes, from the Reformed branch of English Protestantism: correspondingly, it was the Puritan and the type of Anglican more likely to identify with the Protestant Reformation who produced the body of material this book is based on.

16 According to John N. King, this shared literary tradition had origins in the sixteenth century: 'The Protestant poetics that emerged during the reign of Edward VI generated a common literary tradition capable of accommodating minor differences between the literary modes of later Anglicans and Puritans. Virtually all Protestant authors absorbed the cadences of both the Tudor Bible translations and Cranmer's prayer book and homilies. The legacy of the biblical and visionary poetics of the earliest Protestant authors may be traced through the writings of John Donne and George Herbert, Henry Vaughan and Thomas Traherne, John Milton and John Bunyan, and even Isaac Watts and William Blake.' *English Reformation Literature: The Tudor Origins of the Protestant Tradition* (Princeton: Princeton University Press, 1982), 7.

17 Sources for this book had the following denominational affiliations: *Anglican*: Richard Allen, Lancelot Andrewes, Lewis Bayly, Arthur Bedford, Nicholas Brady, Joseph Brookbank, Charles Butler, Edmund Calamy, Henry Dodwell, Daniel Featley, John Hall, Joseph Hall, Henry Hare (Lord Coleraine), William Holder, Nathanial Ingelo, Thomas Morley, John Newte, William Perkins, Thomas Ravenscroft, Edward Reynoldes, Michael Sparke, Humphrey Sydenham, James Ussher. *Puritan, Nonconformist*: Thomas Adams, William Ames, Richard Baxter, Robert Bolton, Thomas Bradbury, John Thomas Ford, Benjamin Gravener, William Harris, Nathaniel Homes, Earle Jabez, Benjamin Keach, John Mason, Cotton Mather

The reader will notice that, for the sake of flow and convenience, I have modernized the spelling whenever possible (except in publication titles). I have, however, tried to keep punctuation and capitalization true to the original, printed sources.

(colonial), John Newman, John Owen, John Preston, Thomas Reynolds, Francis Rous, Richard Sibbes, Isaac Watts, George Wither. In some cases (Preston, Perkins, and Calamy, for example) a precise identification is difficult.

Chapter One

The State of Singing in England *c.* 1575-1710

'But supper being ended and music books (according to the custom)
being brought to the table, the mistress of the house presented me with a
part earnestly requesting me to sing; but when, after many excuses, I
protested unfeignedly that I could not, every one began to wonder …'
—Thomas Morley, *A Plain and Easy Introduction to Practical Music*

When we think of this period, we are irresistibly drawn to its vocal music.
Early modern England represents a golden age for singers. Beginning with
the lutenist school, Dowland, Morley, Campion, Bartlett, Pilkington, Attey,
and others crystallized the passions of loss and lament into exquisite
miniatures at the same time that a tradition of madrigal writing arose which
competed with the Italian for its word-painting inventiveness. Tallis,
Gibbons, and Byrd composed profound vocal works for both cathedral and
private chamber. During the seventeenth century, the brothers Henry and
William Lawes devoted their energies to continuo song; and our period
culminates with Henry Purcell, whose vocal writing merged the traditional
English textual sensitivity with a florid Italianate style, and who would
have probably been an even greater innovative figure in western music if
not for his premature death at the age of thirty-six. These are some of the
names which comprise the surface of a nation's musical life. Yet
underneath this surface other, perhaps less-obvious, social factors were also
at work, in the form of three musical traditions which made their own
unique contributions to the art of English singing. Before examining the
symbolic significance of the human voice within the period's devotional
culture, it will be helpful to first identify these traditions, and the milieus,
both amateur and professional, where vocal performance typically
occurred.

The first stream, the English cathedral music school tradition,
represented sophistication and learning, and was that force largely
responsible for transmitting musical theory and practice as it had been
formulated throughout the great ecclesiastical and intellectual centers of
Europe. Based as it was upon early Christian chant, what we now call
western art, or classical, music had originally derived from a religious and
theological context; and, appropriately enough, the church continued to be
an important patron of musical activity in England throughout the sixteenth
and seventeenth centuries. While the secular genres of masque and theater

blossomed under the Stuarts, and competed for the best performers and composers, the fact that, even at the end of the seventeenth century, the most prominent contemporary names in English composition—Purcell, Blow, Humfrey and Croft—had all cut their musical teeth, so to speak, at the Chapel Royal, first as 'children,' and then as 'gentlemen,' shows the persistent influence of the church's educational legacy upon professional musicians in this culture.

This legacy faced serious disruptions in the form of structural change in both the sixteenth and seventeenth centuries. Henry VIII's willingness to break from the Roman institutional church affected the training and education of singers during the early Reformation period. Ideas have consequences, and in this case they had musical ones. When English monasteries were suppressed in the years 1538-1540, the attached song schools were also abolished, and many 'singing men' had to look for new ways to make a living. Beyond the monasteries, the church had also traditionally supported town and village elementary schools, or chantries, where local boys were taught the fundamentals of music, along with grammar and writing. An act by Henry VIII in 1547 closed over two thousand of these schools, and left only a few major centers open, in Oxford, Cambridge, St. George's Chapel at Windsor, the court's Chapel Royal, and the colleges of Winchester and Eton.[1] Still more disruptions came in the next century, as the wartime Parliament abolished sung services in 1644 and traditional Anglican cathedral worship ceased entirely by 1647. The former pattern of musical activity in England's ecclesiastical centers would not resume until Charles II inherited his father's throne a decade and a half later.[2]

Yet this particular vocal tradition proved a resilient one. Although the monastic schools and town chantries were decimated in the 1540s, musical life in the cathedrals continued on with much the same strength as it had before the Reformation; sung services occurred daily, and the schools attached to these institutions continued to train young singers. The shift in theology did necessitate some changes: previous repertory lauding the Virgin and saints required alterations; Latin prayers were passed over in favor of texts in the English vernacular; and the old Mass was streamlined. Paradoxically, what might appear to have been a huge systemic blow to the cause of music did contain the seed of creative possibilities; for one, composers now had more flexibility in choosing biblical texts and subject matter. The new Church of England prescribed rites of varying musical

---

1 Iain Fenlon, 'Education in music: Renaissance and Reformation Schools,' in *The New Grove Dictionary of Music and Musicians.*
2 The musical changes in Anglican parish churches during this time were less dramatic than in the cathedrals: see Ruth M. Wilson, *Anglican Chant and Chanting in England, Scotland, and America* (Oxford: Clarendon Press, 1996).

complexity: 'short services' generally contain simple, homophonic choral settings, while 'great services' feature more elaborate polyphonic textures and grander instrumentation. The Anglican church would become known for its anthems (free-standing choral pieces inserted within the liturgy), and Byrd, Tallis, Gibbons, Purcell, Blow, and Croft all contributed substantively to this repertory. English composers probably found the form of the verse anthem, a variation originating in the late sixteenth century, especially appealing on account of its expanded forces of soloist, chorus, organ, and other instruments. All of these liturgical reforms, codified during this era, established a tone and style to Anglican worship which continues to this day.

Cathedral schools began training young boys at the ages of six to seven. As being a professional church musician was often associated with taking holy orders of some sort, only boys and men participated. The curriculum at these schools was comprehensive and designed to produce knowledgeable participants in the Anglican liturgy. Choristers learned the rules of consonance and dissonance, and sight-singing according to the *gamut*, an intricate system of syllables and hexachords which originated with Guido d'Arezzo in the eleventh century. In the days before printed books were common, music education was chiefly an oral tradition which relied upon repetition and memorization of the large chant repertory. After the Reformation, this oral approach seems to have diminished somewhat in favor of a new emphasis upon reading 'pricksong,' or musical notation. Ancient chant was also losing its hegemony because English composers preferred to concentrate on the new anthem form.[3] Nevertheless, remnants of the old unwritten tradition lingered in descant, the technique of singing two and three-part counterpoint above a given cantus firmus. Training of the youngest students still depended upon methods which did not call for advanced reading skills. Thomas Morley's *A Plain and Easy Introduction to Practical Music* (1597) implies that descant remained an oral, improvisatory art well into the Protestant era with its directions 'now I pray you set me a plainsong and I will try how I can sing upon it'; also, with its anecdote of the tutor who sang plainsongs on walks accompanied by descanting pupils.[4] Shades of medieval chant tradition also appear in Anglican chant, a distinct feature of the Church of England liturgy.[5]

---

3 A shift in focus in the training of English choristers, from improvisation to reading notation, appeared under Elizabeth I (*c.* 1565). See Jan Flynn, 'The Education of Choristers in England During the Sixteenth Century,' in *English Choral Practice 1400-1658*, John Morehen, ed. (Cambridge University Press: 1995).

4 Thomas Morley, *A Plaine and Easie Introduction to Practicall Musicke* (London, 1597), 120.

5 See Wilson, *Anglican Chant.*

The tonal ideal for cathedral singers combined purity, clarity, and flexibility. Although most English service music from the sixteenth and seventeenth centuries did not demand the same level of vocal *fioritura* as the Italian repertory, choristers still needed sufficient skill to negotiate melismatic passages with ease: a skill undoubtedly learned through example and repetition. To a listener, the most obvious aural characteristic of English sacred music remains the 'hooty' or hollow tone which pre-pubescent boys naturally produce, and which the excellent resonating quality of cathedral architecture serves to emphasize. So apparently enamored are the English with this timbre, in fact, that it continues to define the nation's choral sound to this day; and professional women choristers in England are frequently expected to straighten their tone and omit their natural vibrato in order to replicate this boyish quality—a practice not without its detractors, for it is a technique believed by some to strain the mature female voice.

In contrast to the relatively small number of English singers who trained in the cathedral system, the second stream beckoned to all segments of society: men and women, children and servants, old and young, rich and poor. This was the popular psalm-singing culture, which shared many things in common with the informal music tradition of carols, drinking songs, sea chanties, spinning and weaving songs, and broadside ballads. The Puritans are famous for their enthusiastic psalmody, but it is less well known that it flourished in Anglican circles as well; indeed, congregational singing led by a parish clerk was often the only form of church music heard in humbler towns and villages. This populist tradition had its parallel to cathedral boy choristers in the form of 'charity children,' choirs of poor children from local grammar schools who led psalm-singing in town parishes.[6] Psalm-singing consequently touched large numbers of the population during the early modern era, and it became a moral and political, as well as musical, force to be reckoned with.

We unfortunately have few indicators of actual performance practice of the metrical psalm literature. References to 'Geneva jigs' in the sixteenth century indicate that tempos could be quite lively, at least in the early years of the Reformation. Over time, however, congregational singing generally sunk to a slower pace, a tendency exacerbated by the practice of 'lining out,' where a clerk reads each phrase before it is sung (used in cases where sufficient psalters were unavailable, or the congregation illiterate). Isaac Watts' plea for faster tempos suggests that these conditions continued into the early eighteenth century. Unaccompanied singing tended to stray out of tune as well: as Thomas Mace lamented, ''Tis sad to hear what whining, toting, yelling, or screeking, there is in many Country congregations, as if

---

6   For more on metrical psalmody in Anglican parish churches, see ibid.

the people were affrighted or distracted.'[7] A reform movement subsequently arose during the late seventeenth century among English ministers hoping to revive musical literacy in their congregations, and *The Accomplished Singer* was written in the midst of a similar impulse in the American colonies in the early eighteenth century. Its author, Cotton Mather, was apparently writing from sad experience when he described some congregational singing which had degenerated into an 'odd noise':

> They must have strange Notions of the divine Spirit, and of His Operations, who shall imagine, that the Delight which their Untuned Ears take in an Uncouth Noise, more than in a Regular Singing, is any Communion with Him ... Regular Singing must needs be Better than the confused Noise of a Wilderness.[8]

Many Protestant divines were actually quite sensitive about the problem of poor singing from their congregations; and, although a sincere heart mattered infinitely more in their scheme of things than a brilliant technique, they were not entirely averse to the acquisition of 'artificial skills' through musical training. Isaac Watts noted, for example, that Christians should take 'all the advantages that nature can obtain' in communicating the gospel. Given the tendency of hearts to wander, he calls it 'a necessary duty to know and avoid those disagreeable ways of pronunciation, that may rather disgust than edify such as may join us.'[9] The benefit of singing musically and thus improving every talent to its best advantage was bolstered by appeals to I Cor. 6:20, 'glorify God in your body.' Here the Presbyterian minister John Newman, preaching in a series of reformist lectures on the subject of singing at the Weighhouse in Eastcheap *c.* 1708, reveals the reaction of his psalm-singing culture to the growing vocal professionalism abroad at that time in England:

> I would not be thought to discourage those from this Duty who have little or no artificial skill; many can sing in conjunction with others, though they can't lead a Tune: and they that have not so much Skill as this, may so manage their Voices, as not to disturb those that have, and by joining with them may be greatly affected and edified much more perhaps than

---

7 Thomas Mace, *Musick's Monument: or, a Rembrancer Of the Best Practical Musick, Both Divine, and Civil, that has ever been known, to have been in the World* (London, 1676), 9.

8 Cotton Mather, *The Accomplished Singer, Instructions How the Piety of Singing with a True Devotion, may be obtained and expressed; the Glorious God after an uncommon manner Glorified in it, and His people Edified* (Boston, 1721), 22. Appearing the same year as Thomas Walter's *The Grounds and Rules of Musick explained*, Mather's treatise served as an apology for the musical reforms proposed by Walter; Mather also signed the preface to Walter's book.

9 Isaac Watts, 'Of the Tone of the Voice in Prayer,' in *The Beauties of the late Reverend Dr. Isaac Watts* (London, 1782), 146.

those who have ten times their Skill, but want their pious Dispositions of Soul. Though still I am of opinion, that if such Christians have a natural Capacity for it, some artificial Skill would be very serviceable to them, in the more Spiritual Performance of the Duty.[10]

So it is obvious that this type of performance ranged widely in quality, and its success depended largely upon the natural gifts of the singers at hand. Albeit lacking the finesse of the cathedral tradition, popular devotional singing did have many attractive qualities, for at its best it represented the soul of a culture striving earnestly to experience a type of spiritual comfort and beauty, often in the midst of desperate circumstances.

The movement's democratic impulses, moreover, associate it with another facet of English musical life which eventually took on a life of its own. The popularity of psalm-singing brought the challenge of musical literacy for the masses, and during this period we begin to see a new category of books written exclusively for the musical novice. Notably, it was the psalter editors back in the sixteenth century who first addressed this problem by inserting rudiments of theory and sightsinging into their copies. The third edition of Sternholde's *The first part of the Psalmes collected into English Meter* (1564) offered

A short introduction into the Science of Music, made for such as are desirous to have the knowledge thereof for the singing of these Psalms ... whereby (any diligence given thereunto) every man in a few days, yea in a few hours, easily without all pain, and that also without aid or help of any other teacher, attain to a sufficient knowledge to sing any Psalm contained in this book.[11]

Sightsinging was presented in terms of *fasola*, a simplified solmization system derived from the old gamut. The habit of including instructional prologues (up to thirty pages long) in mass-produced psalters continued throughout the era: this represented, save for the occasional singing class by an itinerant music master, the primary form of music education for town and village dwellers. In time, similar didactic goals prompted the publication of several English titles, including Bathe's *Briefe Introduction to the Skill of Song* (1596), Morley's *Plaine and Easie Introduction to Practicall Musicke* (1597), Dowland's translation of Andreas Ornithoparcus's *Micrologus, or Introduction: Containing the Art of Singing* (1609), Ravenscroft's *A Briefe Discourse* (1614), Butler's *The Principles of Musik* (1636), John Playford's *Brief Introduction to the Skill of Musick*

---

10 John Newman, 'Directions for the right Performance of the Duty of Singing,' in *Practical Discourses of Singing*, 159.

11 Esther Abrams Landon, 'Seventeenth and Eighteenth Century and Colonial American Music Texts: An Analysis of Instructional Content' (Ph.D. diss., University of California Los Angeles, 1977), 15.

(1654), Simpson's *A Compendium of Practical Musick* (1667), and Mace's *Musick's Monument* (1676). While the writings of Morley, Dowland, Ravenscroft, and Butler assumed a more sophisticated tone than the psalter prefaces, the tremendous popularity of *A Brief Introduction to the Skill of Musick*, which underwent twenty-two editions between 1654 and 1730 (Burney claimed that it was 'more generally purchased and read than any elementary musical tract that ever appeared in this or any other country'),[12] was due largely to Playford's simplified approach to music education, a legacy of the Protestant psalter.

These works spend tantalizingly little time discussing actual vocal production. Even those by Bathe and Dowland (which contain *singing* in their titles) equate knowing 'how to sing' with a familiarity of the basic rules of music theory—perhaps reflecting the traditional bias for the *musicus*, a musical scholar versed in the liberal arts, over the *cantus*, a mere performer. Amateurs who sang sacred and secular songs did not bother too much with problems of technique, or trouble themselves with wondering whether or not they had good voices in the first place. Like eating and breathing, singing was considered a natural act which one simply *did:* the concept of the virtuoso would later spring from an entirely different, continental musical tradition (see below). But Dowland's translation of *Micrologus* does offer Ornithoparcus's observation about regional styles of singing in the sixteenth century:

> Every man lives after his own humor; neither are all men governed by the same laws, and divers Nations have divers fashions, and differ in habit, diet, studies, speech, and song. Hence is it, that the English do carol; the French sing; the Spaniards weep; the Italians, which dwell about the Coasts of *Ianua* caper with their Voices; the other bark: but the Germans (which I am ashamed to utter) do howl like Wolves.[13]

While we might wish that the German scholar had been more descriptive on the subject of English singers, at least he did not insult them by comparing them to dogs or wolves!

As in Continental writings from this period, common sense prevails in English sources on the subject of vocal technique.[14] Some manuals provide

---

12 Charles Burney, *A General History of Music from the Earliest Ages to the Present Period* (London, 1782-9), 2:417.

13 *Andreas Ornithoparcus His Micrologus, or Introduction: Containing the Art of Singing*, John Dowland, tr. (London, 1609), 88. Elsewhere Ornithoparchus jibes: 'Why the Saxons, and those that dwell upon the Baltic coast, should so delight in such clamouring, there is no reason, but either because they have a deaf God, or because they think he is gone to the South-side of heaven, and therefore cannot so easily hear both the Easterlings, and the Southerlings.' 90.

14 See Don Harran, 'Directions to singers in writings of the early Renaissance,' *Revue belge de musicology* 41 (1987): 45-61.

vocalises in the form of scales and simple intervallic passages. Singers are advised to watch their posture, pay attention to the rhythm, articulate the words of the text clearly and not distort the vowels (Morley: 'study how to vowel and sing clean'), maintain a pleasant and inoffensive manner, and, in sum, avoid doing anything ridiculous or exaggerated which would draw attention to oneself: gasping for breath, letting the tongue fall out of one's mouth, bulging the eyes, overextending the jaw, etc. Playford's treatise offers somewhat more technical detail: 'In the expressing of your Voice, or Tuning of Notes, let the Sound come clear from your throat, and not through your teeth, by sucking in your breath, for that is a great obstruction to the clear utterance of the Voice.'[15] Certain concepts about the benefits of singing are frequently mentioned as well. Singing is the best type of music, for it is natural and ancient; it is also good for the health. Henry Peacham in *The Complete Gentleman* cites that it 'openeth the breast and pipes' and is a 'great lengthener of life.' Playford agrees that it 'doth clear and strengthen the Lungs, and if it be also joined the Exercise of the Limbs, none need fear Asthma or Consumption.' Both claim that singing corrects bad pronunciation, stammering, and other speech defects. In sum, singing is presented as a good and wholesome activity for both amateurs and professionals—and woe to that gentleman like Thomas Morley who could not hold up his end at music parties! With such scanty technical advice, the average Englishman and woman felt sufficiently equipped to 'sing it and chant it.'[16]

   In contrast to these two native musical traditions, an entirely different approach to vocal training and performance was brought to Stuart-era London by the growing number of foreign musicians who made it home.[17] This was the Italian singing culture, which must have fairly oozed exotic appeal to English sophisticates tired of the same old 'beef and ale.' The Italian style of music in general grew markedly in popularity between the years 1660 and 1770. Taking its cue from the court, London society increasingly aspired to the cultivated continental manner of painting,

---

15 John Playford, *A Brief Introduction to the Skill of Music* (London, 1674), 20.

16 While we know that singers of Elizabethan and Jacobean lute songs were schooled in musical-rhetorical gestures and embellishments (see Toft), I do not count it as a separate vocal culture, because it was a style within an art music tradition which ultimately owed its existence to the cathedral educational system.

17 The two predominant styles of classical singing during this time were the Italian and the French, and England adopted the Italian manner. Quantz contrasted the two in 1752: 'The Italian manner of singing is refined and full of art; it moves us and at the same time excites our admiration, it has the spirit of music, it is pleasant, charming, expressive, rich in the taste and feeling, and it carries the hearer agreeably from one passion to another. The French manner of singing is more plain than full of art, more speaking than singing: the expression of the passions and the voice is more strange than natural.' See *Groves* article s.v. 'Singing.'

architecture, theater, dress, and music. This era was one of a growing stratification: while aristocrats and would-be aristocrats typically preferred Italian and French styles, the humbler classes remained loyal to traditional English styles of music and visual art. H. James Jensen notes that this 'great shift in taste' finds a telling record in the Restoration comedies of Thomas Shadwell: '*In Bury Fair*, the refined Bellamy has his musicians perform a two-part Italian song to entertain his guest, and in another scene, when Philadelphia ... sings two Italian songs, the well-bred Gertrude says: " 'Tis admirable! The court has not better." ' Jensen further adds that the only characters in Shadwell's plays who like English songs are 'either ill-bred or stupid, or both.'[18]

Italian musicians were usually Roman Catholic, and hence excluded from participation in the official Chapel Royal, but they could be hired for the king's personal amusement and court entertainments, as well as for the chapels and private devotions of the Catholic queens Henrietta Maria and Catherine of Braganza. Indeed, the record shows that by the latter half of the seventeenth century these singers had comfortably established their presence in such contexts. The *Angliae notitia* indicates that when Catherine first heard mass at the Friary Chapel at St. James in 1662, alongside the officiating Portuguese priests were 'divers persons belonging to the Music of the Chapel, as well Italians as Portuguese, and others to serve at the Altar.'[19] During the reign of James II, Italian singers ('Gregorians') gained more prominence as they staffed the new Catholic chapel at Whitehall, where they sang to the amazement of onlookers, prompting John Evelyn to observe with Anglican dismay:

> I heard the famous Cifeccio (Eunuch) sing, in the new popish chapel this afternoon, which was indeed very rare, and with great skill: He came over from Rome, esteemed one of the best voices in Italy, much crowding, little devotion.[20]

In the same year Evelyn also records:

> I was to hear the music of the Italians in the new Chapel ... Nothing can be finer than the magnificent marble work and Architecture at the end ... the work of Mr. Gibbons ... [A] world of mysterious Ceremony the music

---

18 H. James Jensen, 'English Restoration Attitudes Towards Music,' *The Musical Quarterly* 55 (1969): 206 *passim*.

19 E. Chamberlayne, *Angliae notitia* (London, 1669); quoted in John Harley, *Music in Purcell's London: The Social Background* (London: Dennis Dobson, 1968), 93.

20 John Evelyn, *Diaries*, E.S. deBeer, ed. (London: Oxford University Press, 1959), January 30, 1686. Siface, or Giovanni Francesco Grossi, joined the Catholic chapel royal in 1687 upon invitation by Maria of Modena. He was already renowned as a sacred oratorio singer at San Marcello's in Rome, had sung at the Neapolitan opera house, and was a favourite of Queen Christina of Sweden.

playing and singing: and so I came away: not believing I should ever have lived to see such things in the K. of England's palace, after it had pleas'd God to enlighten this nation.[21]

Besides their activities at court, émigré singers gave lessons and performed in the country estates and town houses of the wealthy: practices which strengthened the ascendancy of Italian music in English society. The Italian singer Pietro Reggio, who lived in England from 1664, was one such tutor; in 1678 his treatise on vocal ornamentation entitled *The Art of Singing* was published.[22] Evelyn's daughter Mary studied singing with him and harpsichord with Bartolomeo Albrici. Samuel Pepys hired a musician named Morelli to play the lute and sing for domestic entertainment after the Restoration.

The Italian approach to singing was crystallized in several treatises written around the turn of the seventeenth century and contained within music editions: Zacconi's *Prattica di musica utile et necessaria si al compositore si anco al cantare* (1592); Bovicelli's *Regole, passaggi di musica, madrigali e motetti passaggiati* (1594); Caccini's *Nuove Musiche* (1601); and Severi's *Salmi Passaggiati* (1615). These and similar works describe a method whose goal is the realization of 'il cantar di gorga' (singing with the throat) through mastery of *passaggi*, or melodic ornamentation. This aesthetic derived from regional traditions which had flourished for quite some time, for a propensity for florid ornament is found in the sixteenth-century forms of canzonetta, aria, bergamasche, *veneziane*, and *napolitane*.[23] The Italian method was learned chiefly through imitation of a skilled teacher, so it was highly labor-intensive, and personality-centered as well. In order to negotiate *fioratura* successfully, a singer must have complete control of his or her instrument; the *exclamatio*, for example—a swelling and decreasing of a sustained note—requires firm breath support and secure placement of the tone within the resonating cavities. In these treatises we encounter the beginnings of a more anatomical approach towards vocal technique, with mention of the throat, uvula, teeth, tongue, etc.; they fostered a fresh emphasis on the voice and its

---

21 Ibid., December 29, 1686.
22 It is not extant.
23 According to Howard Meyer Brown, these early Italian songs 'became vehicles for demonstrating to appreciative audiences how skillful solo singers could be in varying their embellishments from strophe to strophe.' He sees a direct influence of this regional *fioratura* tradition upon Caccini courtesy of the composer's relationship with the voice teacher Scipione del Palla: 'The association of these two musicians [Caccini and del Palla] makes clear how closely Caccini's art of singing and of composition was connected with the quasi-popular unwritten tradition.' Howard Meyer Brown, 'The Geography of Florentine Monody,' *Early Music 9* (1981): 154, 158.

potential which in turn signalled the birth of a new professional class of European singers.[24]

The first English translation of an Italian vocal treatise appeared in 1664, when John Playford included portions of *Le Nuove Musiche* in his *A Brief Introduction to the Skill of Musick* under the title 'A Brief Discourse of the Italian manner of Singing.' Here Caccini (translated through an anonymous 'English gentleman') essentially describes the philosophy of the Florentine Camerata: that singing should primarily move the passions of hearers through 'an understanding of the conceit and the humor of the words.' He follows this with an explanation of the trill, *gruppo*, and *exclamatio*, and describes the appeal of a well-placed rubato, 'that excellent kind of singing with a graceful neglect.' The postscript hints of the extent to which Italian singing methods were changing traditional English practice. While acknowledging that the Italian language is 'more smooth and better vowell'd than the English,' and thus better for singing, it counters,

> Yet of late years our Language is much more refined, and so is our Music to a more smooth and delightful way and manner of singing after this new method; especially by the excellent Compositions of Mr. Henry Lawes, and other excellent Masters in this Art, and by them taught above this forty years ...

Finally, it advises aspiring singers that they 'need not seek after Italian or French Masters,' but may engage English tutors with the fullest confidence that they, too, are now expert in this art.

By the early eighteenth century the Italian singing culture had firmly entrenched itself within the London music scene. A production of *Camilla* by Bononcini opened in 1706 to great success; and the first entirely sung Italian opera performed in England, Handel's *Rinaldo*, premiered in 1711 at the Queen's Theatre. But the same era also witnessed an English backlash against this new art form.[25] One early reaction appeared the same year as *Camilla* (1706), when John Dennis in his *Essay on the Operas after the Italian Manner* denounced opera for being soft and effeminate, a 'diversion of pernicious consequences,' an 'invasion of foreign luxury,' and, in short, the product of a nation of men who are 'neither virtuous, nor wise, nor valiant.' London 'people of quality,' he complained, now encourage this staged nonsense in lieu of their own comedies and tragedies.

---

24 H. Wiley Hitchcock: 'It was an art that rested on a foundation of absolute mastery of the voice, a virtuoso-level proficiency perhaps difficult for us even to imagine.' Introduction of *Le Nuove Musiche*, H. Wiley Hitchcock, ed. (Madison, Wisconsin: A-R Editions Inc. 1970), 10.

25 Recent scholarship has focused upon the connection between English opera criticism and eighteenth-century nationalism. See Ruth Smith, *Handel's Oratorios and Eighteenth-Century Thought* (Cambridge: Cambridge University Press, 1995).

Even though such critiques were to remain a feature of Georgian literary culture, the Italian approach to vocal technique grew in favor throughout the 18th century, and gained status as being the most effective, specialized, and professional method available anywhere. Two documents from the period exemplify how quickly this foreign vocal aesthetic was being absorbed into the English consciousness. The first, Peter Prelleur's attractively-illustrated treatise *The Modern Musick-Master* (1731), devotes separate sections to theory, sight singing, the *hautbois,* and the German flute, as well as other popular instruments. While its 'Introduction to Singing' lacks advice on actual vocal technique, it does contain arias from *Julius Caesar*, *Theseus*, and *Tamerlane*, thus assuming a strong interest in Italian opera and a fairly accomplished level of skill among its readers. A decade later, in 1742, J.E. Galliard presented an English translation of Pietro Tosi's 1723 treatise, *Observations on the Florid Song; or Sentiments on the Ancient and Modern Singer*. One who reads this gains a sense that the Italian vocal culture has truly arrived in England. In his pithy style, Tosi covers the same general territory as Caccini, but adds the subjects of vocal registers, stage presence, recitative, the *appoggiatura*, and *portamento*.

Continental tradition also had much to do with the era's growing acceptance of professional female singers. While there are indications that English society was changing its attitude on this point through the seventeenth century—a Mrs. Edward Coleman sung in Davenant's *Entertainment at Rutland House* and *Siege of Rhodes* in 1656, for example, and various other women had performed in public as well[26]—it was the tolerant practicality of the Italian opera culture which finally clinched the matter. So in 1710 we have the *donnas* Isabella Girardeau, Elisabetta Pilotti-Schiavonetti, and Francesca Vanini all appearing together on a London stage in *Rinaldo*: a spectacle virtually impossible to imagine in England a century before. Although it would be some time before controversies over the propriety of women performing in public were resolved to everyone's satisfaction, the pattern was set.

These three vocal cultures within early modern England—the cathedral, psalmodic, and Italian—represent such diverse contexts that one rightly questions the extent of any mutual engagement. At the very least, it is clear that singing touched English lives in all segments of society, and was a primary form of entertainment in a simpler age. Psalms were paramount within the Puritan movement: the divines cited throughout this book were steeped in the psalmodic tradition, and these simple melodies were the sonorities which formed their primary musical landscape. Anglican leaders knew their metrical Psalms too, but they were also products of a

---

26 I.e., Mrs. Ayliff, Mrs. Knight (who, according to Evelyn, had the 'greatest reach of any English woman'), Charlotte Butler, Arabella Hunt, Anne Bracegirdle, and Laetitia Cross.

sophisticated cathedral tradition, and likely to have been exposed to the new Italianate style as well. We may conclude, then, that the word 'singing' as used by our sources was primarily understood in the context of the two native English traditions which share a sacred subject matter: the psalmodic and cathedral.

Yet it is not true that these three vocal cultures had absolutely nothing to say to each other. Over the course of two centuries they were to merge gradually and blend, shaping the nature and direction of English music through a type of Hegelian dialectic. This interplay is found in the 1674 edition of *An Introduction to the Skill of Musick*. That John Playford was a canny observer of the London scene is apparent through his business relationships with both royalists and Puritans during the civil war, and he applied this acumen to his musical publications as well. *The Skill of Music* is a remarkable document as it addresses all three vocal cultures simultaneously. Alongside 'A Brief Discourse of the Italian Manner of Singing,' the reader finds familiar psalm tunes in 'Rules and Directions for Singing the Psalms,' plus a clear reference to the cathedral tradition, 'The Order of Performing the Divine Service in Cathedrals and Collegiate Chapels.' All three traditions would also show up later in Handel's sacred oratorios, which joined vocal fireworks with sacred and biblical themes, all of it made possible by an art music establishment which owed its very existence to the cathedral tradition. The fact that *Messiah* combines such important signifiers from the musical culture in so winning a manner undoubtedly accounts for its popular reception during Handel's lifetime. Eighteenth-century audiences sensed, quite rightly, that they were witnessing a new creative synthesis. Their enjoyment was all the more enhanced because they brought with them, to varying degrees, a consciousness of the transcendent meaning of the human voice which was their English theological inheritance—and to which we now turn.

Chapter Two

Applying the Word

'On Monday next, he received his sentence of death, after which time he was with the other condemned Prisoners, and did pray with them four times a day, and read to them, and sung Psalms with them.'[1]
—*A Murder Punished and Pardoned*

'I went to Thomas Holly's and William Chadocke's to buy swine's grass, which I did, and when I came home I was very pensive and sad in consideration of my poverty, and I sung the twenty-fourth Psalm, and after I was very hearty. God will comfort and supply the wants of his poor servants ...'[2]
—*The Diary of Roger Lowe*

'We had ... a Custom at Our Meetings, that commonly ... we did Conclude All, with some Vocal Music ... The Best which we did ever Esteem, were Those Things which were most Solemn, and Divine ... Wonderfully Rare, Sublime, and Divine, beyond all Expression.'[3]
—Thomas Mace, *Musick's Monument*

'The master of the ship shut ninety-nine of us under deck in a very small room where we could not lay ourselves down without lying one upon another ... Though we were shut down in the dark as in a dungeon, yet we did pray, and sing praises to our God, and he was a light round about us: objects of pity we were, and arguments from misery to mercy; we had enough in the day to behold the miserable sight of botches, pox, others devoured with lice till they were almost at death's door.'[4]
—John Coad, *A Memorandum of the Wonderful Providences of God*

---

1 *A Murder Punished and Pardoned, or a True Relation of the Wicked Life, and Shameful-happy death of Thomas Savage, Imprisoned, justly Condemned, and twice Executed at Ratcliff, for his Bloody Fact in Killing his Fellow-Servant* (London, 1668); quoted in Dewey D. Wallace, Jr., ed., *The Spirituality of the Later English Puritans* (Macon, Georgia: Mercer University Press, 1987), 87.

2 William L. Sachse, ed., *The Diary of Roger Lowe of Ashton-in-Makerfield, Lancashire, 1663-1674* (New Haven: Yale University Press, 1938); quoted in Treacy, 153.

3 Mace, *Musick's Monument*, 235.

4 John Coad, *A Memorandum of the Wonderful Providences of God to a poor unworthy Creature, during the time of the Duke of Monmouth's Rebellion and to the Revolution in 1688* (London: Longman, Brown, Green and Longmans, 1849), 23.

The Word

It is common knowledge that, like their spiritual kin on the Continent, English Protestants in the early modern period emphasized the role of the Bible as both divine revelation and practical guide. Rejecting the medieval reliance upon religious images and visual art as 'books for the simple,' they rather encouraged popular literacy and Bible-reading as the chief means of transmitting the faith. Cultures heavily influenced by Reformation ideals, such as England, historically tended to channel their energies into more abstract arts like literature and music, which carried (at least in popular estimation) less danger of idolatry—a sin which elicited an enormous amount of attention during this era. The world-view in which these arts of the mind developed was ripe with dramatic possibilities. For a Christian's life on earth was regarded as a journey through a strange land, an epic battle between the forces of good and evil which took place not only in the public sphere, but in the inner psyche as well; consequently, the individual heart gained renewed attention as the locus of spiritual responsibility.[5] While the notorious iconoclasm of the sixteenth and seventeenth centuries would seem to indicate an ignorant and pervasive anti-aestheticism, the religious temper of the age, with its tendency toward interiorizing the spiritual life and its telescoping of the infinite into the finite, carried some profound artistic implications as well.[6] For if original sin and divine grace were true, and if heaven and hell represented real and terrifyingly inescapable destinations—as many, if not most, English men and women of the time believed—then every person played a lead role in *the* play of ultimate importance; and the individual working out of this moral drama subsequently became a matter of great creative interest for poets, composers, librettists, and dramatists.

The opening quotes to this chapter are but a few which tell of the extent singing accompanied a wide range of personal experience in early modern England—from the grind of daily life to those rarefied moments when existence itself hangs in the balance. Its ubiquity in the written record of diaries, letters, memoirs, and histories transcends the narrower denominational boundaries of Anglican, Independent, Presbyterian, Congregational, Baptist, *et al*. The significance credited to singing by this confessing culture is remarkable, and resonates across time to move and

---

5   Early English Protestantism stressed self-examination, personal abasement, and repentance after the manner of the *Confessions*, and so was a variety of that Augustinian devotionalism which had undergone ebbs and flows throughout the centuries; the writings of Bernard of Clairveaux, for example, exhibit a similar strain of piety of the medieval era.

6   See William A. Dyrness, *Reformed Theology and Visual Culture: the Protestant Imagination from Calvin to Edwards* (Cambridge: Cambridge University Press, 2004).

touch us even today. While the layers of meaning surrounding the human voice in English society were many and complex, the first to be examined is perhaps the most fundamental one: the connection between singing and theological interest in the concept of the Word—which, in the heavily Christianized culture that was early modern England, was universally understood to mean, in its most transcendent sense, God's word, the Bible. While much as been written about the logocentric bent of early modern England, few have recognized its implications upon the period's sociology of vocal performance.

'The Word is like the salve: conviction of conscience is like the laying on of the salve; meditation the binding of it to the sore,'[7] stated the popular seventeenth-century devotional author William Fenner in *The Use and Benefit of Divine Meditation*. The deep interest in scripture evidenced here was not limited to Fenner's Puritan circle: it was shared by all English Protestants. The Anglican bishop James Ussher,[8] for example, echoed Fenner's metaphor in his treatise *A Method for Meditation*:

> To meditate, one hour spent thus is more worth than a thousand sermons, and this is no debasing of the word, but an honour unto it. Thus the word is particularly applied, laid home: Our preaching is but reading of a lecture. A Physician that reads a lecture in the Schools, touching the curing of an ague, his reading will never do it, yet it is necessary we should have the way to cure it, yet that doth it not, the medicine must be applied, such a Dose, etc., So in Preaching, the same word heard in public, the same word applied; every one must spread the Plaster on his own heart.[9]

Seventeenth-century English divines such as Fenner and Ussher liked to write about the Word in all of its forms: written, spoken, and sung. As song usually involved a text, these ideas undergirded the era's regard for the power of the singing voice. Certainly a high esteem for the word's potentialities was not unique to Protestantism: Plato had exposed similar ideas over a thousand years earlier in pre-Christian Athens; and, closer to our period, Italian musical humanism had been experimenting with the concept of textual primacy for decades (the *seconda prattica*), inventing along the way, almost incidentally, the genres of oratorio and opera. Indeed, music in such contexts was commonly referred to as *imitazione della parola*—'imitation of the word.' In early modern England, however, we have a somewhat different situation, for as logocentrism reached a wider range of the society through best-selling devotional and theological works,

---

7   William Fenner, *The Use and Benefit of Divine Meditation* (London, 1657), 4.

8   Best-known today for his speculations about the age of the earth.

9   James Ussher, *A Method for Meditation; or, A Manuall of Divine Duties* (London, 1657), 43.

no longer were such discussions limited to an intellectual elite; further, since this mind-set was tied so closely to deeply-held religious ideals ('the Word'), it arguably affected the culture's collective subconscious in a more profound and intimate way. So when Fenner and Ussher compared the word to a salve with curative properties, they were repeating a theme well-familiar to the average English churchgoer.

Roots of this cultural interest in the word are evident in the writings of the French theologian Jean Calvin, whose comprehensive *Institutes of the Christian Religion* was required reading at English universities by the turn of the seventeenth century. As a reformer, Calvin was simultaneously a product of fifteen centuries of Christian intellectualism and a new voice in the controversial wilderness. He uses 'the Word' to mean, at various times: the eternal decrees of God; the Holy Scriptures; God's *logos*—his wisdom and truth; temporal expressions of this wisdom found in prophecy and preaching; Jesus Christ; and, finally, the standard blocks of human language.[10] While his ideas concerning the word and other topics are at times reminiscent of Augustine, Clement of Alexandria, and other patristic thinkers, he succeeded in returning these fundamental concepts to the fore of theological debate, and gave them a renewed sense of urgency by fitting them to the patterns of sixteenth-century Protestant controversy, addressing his thoughts not only to a privileged caste of scholar-priests, but to the common layman as well.[11]

'We see that word is used for the nod or command of the Son, who is himself the eternal and essential Word of the Father,' declares the *Institutes* after the gospel of John. 'Princes are God's trumpet, and the church is God's organ, but Christ Jesus is his voice,' follows John Donne.[12] For the English Protestant, the Word, while indicating the scriptural text, also referred to the personage of Christ, 'the Word made flesh' according to orthodox doctrine. The Puritan Francis Rous promises that in the Word's pages, 'thine eyes shall see the Teacher himself.'[13] Combining communication with personality, the term itself was complex and fraught with metaphysical possibilities. One doctrine implied by the *logos* is that, just as Christ is eternally constant in his divine nature, the written or spoken Word also exists, and remains the same, beyond the boundaries of time and

---

10 I am indebted to Steve Guthrie on this point.

11 Clement of Alexandria had earlier described Christ as being, simultaneously, 'Word, Song, and Instrument.' *Exhortation to the Greeks,* in Oliver Strunk, ed., *Source Readings in Music History: From Classical Antiquity through the Romantic Era* (New York: W.W. Norton, 1950), 63.

12 *The Sermons of John Donne,* George R. Potter and Evelyn M. Simpson, eds. (Berkeley: University of California Press, 1959), 6:217.

13 Francis Rous, *The Heavenly Academie; or the highest school, Where alone is that highest Teaching, the Teaching of the Heart* (London, 1638), 129.

space. Calvin criticizes any tendency to minimize its power: 'When the Word of God is set before us in the Scriptures, it were certainly most absurd to imagine that it is only a fleeting and evanescent voice, which is sent out into the air, and comes forth beyond God himself, as was the case with the communications made to the patriarchs, and all the prophecies.' Instead, the Word is a lasting entity in itself: 'The reference is rather to the wisdom ever dwelling with God, and by which all oracles and prophecies were inspired.' Going further, Calvin remarkably identifies this wisdom, the Word, as synonymous *with* God: 'Therefore, as all revelations from heaven are duly designated by the title of the Word of God, so the highest place must be assigned to that substantial Word, the source of all inspiration; which, as being liable to no variation, remains for ever one and the same with God, and is God.'[14] Such passages indicate that we are in important territory when it comes to the Reformation understanding of the Word—a territory slightly forbidding and perhaps alien to modern sensibilities.

The topic continued to captivate English Protestants into the next century. The popular Puritan divine Robert Bolton echoes Calvin's view of the word as eternal essence in *The Saints Sure and Perpetuall Guide:* 'The Word may be called Living, because its self is immortal, and lasteth forever; as doth the living and eternal God, the Author of it.'[15] Rous waxes more eloquent in *The Mysticall Marriage* when he describes the symbiosis which was believed to intuitively take place between eternal Word and human soul:

> Such is the harmony and power of harmony between the spirit and the word, that when you hit a spiritual truth in your soul, there will often come a sound, answer and echo from some place in the word agreeable to it. And as the word doth approve this light, so doth this light approve the word. It loves to look on it, it seeth a heavenly wisdom in it, yea it seeth secrets in it; yea many times it will in some short sentence, yea in some single word, find out a Mine of heavenly doctrine, and as at a little crany [fissure] discover a world of divine truths.[16]

Early modern Protestants considered the Word not only constant and eternal, but lively and pro-active as well. A catalyst in conversion, it also guides the process of sanctification. Richard Sibbes, a favorite author of what was then known as 'affectionate divinity,' writes in *The Tender Heart*: 'God through the use of means softens [the heart] by his word: God's word

14 Jean Calvin, *Institutes of the Christian Religion*, Henry Beveridge, tr. (Grand Rapids: Wm. B. Eerdman Publishing Co., 1962), Bk I, 13:115, 116.

15 Robert Bolton, *The Saints Sure and Perpetuall Guide or A Treasure concerning the Word* (London, 1634), 26.

16 Francis Rous, *The Mysticall Marriage, or Experimental Discoveries of the heavenly Marriage betweene a Soule and her Saviour* (London, 1635), 237.

is a hammer to break, and as a fire to melt the hardened heart ...'[17] Such 'holy violence' was held to be a good thing, for according to Augustinian thought the heart is a complacent and treacherous element, in desperate need of being broken or 'overturned.' Echoing Sibbes, Robert Bolton describes the effects of the Word upon the secret life of the soul:

> The Word may be called Living, because [its] self is immortal, and lasteth for ever; as doth the living and eternal God, the Author of it ... but most especially ... it is called *lively*, because it enters with great power and secret insinuation into every part and power both of soul and body: So that as our life is scattered and dispersed into every little part, and least vein in us, and we feel it both in pain and pleasure; even so the virtue of the Word of God pierceth into every member, into the most secret and hidden closet of the heart, either to break and bruise with terror and astonishment the very bones, and crush the sinews of the sinful soul; or to fill them with marrow and fatness, and to refresh the affections of the truly penitent with joy unspeakable, and glorious; God tells us in *Jeremy* that his word is like fire; and therefore it can fully and clearly enlighten our Consciences, and discover unto us the sinfulness of the most lurking and secret thoughts.[18]

This interest in the Word's power represents more than a passing intellectual fad; it is repeated again and again throughout the literature and becomes perhaps the most definitive feature of early English Protestant piety. A treatise written at the end of the seventeenth century, *Scripture Proof for Singing of Scripture Psalms*, confirms that only the Word can 'sanctify us both inwardly and outwardly, both in soul and body, both in thoughts and actions; without which, both inward and outward holiness, no man shall ever see the face of God.'[19]

Thus Reformed doctrine invested the divine Word with many qualities. It was believed eternal, wise, reliable, transcendent, and a great transformer of both individuals and nation states. Indeed, so much was attributed to the Word, and its purposes so inexorable, that the concept takes on a personality of its own in period writings. It may appear remote, even frightening, yet also exhibits the tenderness of a friend who sticks closer than a brother. The era also believed that these two contrasts were perfectly united in the singing of Psalms and other sacred lyrics. Thus a commonplace musical activity became imbued with tremendous

---

17 Richard Sibbes, 'The Tender Heart,' *The Saints' Cordialls* (London, 1637), 8.

18 Bolton, *Perpetuall Guide*, 26. The quote is from Jer. 23:29.

19 E.H., *Scripture Proof for Singing of Scripture Psalms, Hymns and Spiritual Songs: or, An Answer to several Queries and Objections frequently made use of to stumble and turn aside young Christians from their Duty to God in singing of Psalms* (London, 1696), 27.

metaphysical portent. As the Word represented an active, even *magical* force (doctrinal objections to this term aside), devotional singing in early modern England represented, above all else, a supernatural activity, not merely a human one; and when the Word was 'applied' through song, its potential was believed to be fully realized.[20] Along these lines John Cotton argues that 'singing with voices has the preeminence,' as 'uttering the word of God [does] chiefly utter the Spirit of God breathing in it.'[21] In a sermon on Judges 5:20 John Donne allows that 'all the words of God are always sweet in themselves,' but adds that they are sweetest of all 'where the Holy Ghost hath been pleased to set the word of God to Music, and to convey it into a Song.'[22] Sibbes concurs in *Angels Acclamations*: 'The Word signifies singing, as well as praise, it implies praise expressed in that manner, and indeed praising God, it is the best expression of the affection of joy.'[23] For this reason singing became valued throughout English Protestant culture as a special form of meditation which could 'bind the Word to the sore'; and, just as prose and poetry were favored as genres which allowed the religious imagination to flourish, vocal music represented the individual and physical expression of these arts of the mind.

The Word sung was believed to share many of the same characteristics as the spoken and written word. It, too, could plant the seeds of faith: 'The Word of God sung, as well as preached, may be made powerful to Conversion.'[24] Similarly, just as the Word spoken by God never fades but reverberates into eternity, the singing of sacred lyrics was acclaimed as an action which taps into a timeless dimension. In the classic *Laws of Ecclesiastical Polity*, Richard Hooker writes:

> Others may both conveniently and fruitfully use them [hymns] … when any thing is spoken to extol the goodness of God whose mercy endureth for ever, albeit the very particular occasion whereupon it riseth do come no more, yet *the fountain continuing the same*, and yielding other new effects which are but only in some sort proportionable, a small resemblance between the benefits which we and others have received, may serve to make the same words of praise and thanksgiving fit though not equally in all circumstances fit for both …[25] [emphasis added]

The Word (in all its forms of expression) represented a creative force; fertility; a power calling things into being which did not previously exist. In

---

20 It should be noted here that supernatural does not necessarily mean anti- or irrational: perhaps a better term would be super-rational.

21 John Cotton, *Singing of the Psalms a Gospel-Ordinance* (London, 1647), 5.

22 Donne, *Sermons*, 4:179.

23 Richard Sibbes, 'Angel's Acclamations: or, The Nativity of Christ, celebrated by the Heavenly Host,' in *Light from Heaven in four Treatises* (London, 1638), 212.

24 E.H., *Scripture Proof for Singing*, 31.

25 Richard Hooker, *Of the Laws of Ecclesiastical Polity*, 5, 40:3.

Christian early modern England, most people knew the biblical account of creation in Genesis, where God forms the world from the command of his voice. Although the Bible does not specifically mention it, the related idea of *singing* a world into creation is a particularly tempting variation which English divines sometimes adopted: as John Donne preached (long before C.S. Lewis used the image of a singing Lion-Christ in his Narnia series), 'this world begun with a Song.'[26] Isaac Watts—who was a philosopher as well as a pioneer in the hymn-writing movement—develops this relationship further when he explicitly links the Word and singing with creation in this mystical passage from *The Foretaste of Heaven*:

> Did not the angels rejoice at the birth day of this universe, and those morning stars shout for joy at the first appearance of this creation? And what the inhabitants of heaven make their song, may not a holy soul be entertained with it, even to ecstasy and rapture? I behold, says he in divine meditation, I behold this huge structure of the universe rising out of nothing at the voice of his command: I behold the several planets in their various orders set a moving by the same power ... At his command nature exists in all its regions with all its furniture: the beasts, and birds, and fishes in all their forms arise, and at once they obey the several almighty orders he gave, and by the unknown and inconceivable force of such a word they leap out into existence in ten thousand forms ... When all this philosophy is charged into devotion, it must also be transformed into divine and unutterable joy.[27]

The Word in Literature

By now it is evident that this culture focused its affections upon the Word to a degree perhaps unmatched in the history of the church; for, while theologians had certainly written on this topic before, never had so many pondered the Word's ramifications before such a large and responsive public. Given the text-centered nature of this society, it does not surprise us to learn that England during the same period experienced a marked rise in literacy rates. It has been estimated that by the middle of the seventeenth century, one-third of all adult males in England were literate, and in London, perhaps half.[28] A sermon published in 1708 notes with pride that by now the illiterate 'are but few, especially in London, and other Cities

---

26 Donne, *Sermons*, 180.

27 Isaac Watts, 'The Foretaste of Heaven,' in *The World to Come: or Discourses on the Joys or Sorrows of Departed Souls at Death, and the Glory or Terror of the Resurrection* (London, 1738), 258.

28 Lawrence Stone, 'The Educational Revolution in England, 1560-1640,' *Past and Present* 28 (1964): 42-43; Peter Laslett, *The World We Have Lost* (New York, 1965), pp. 194-98; cited in Sommerville, *Popular Religion in Restoration England*, 20.

and Towns, where there are abundant Opportunities, and ordinarily care taken to instruct the Poor to read.'[29] While literacy rates for females probably remained lower than those for men, the theologically-savvy housewife and learned gentlewoman both made an impact within the culture—there is every indication that early English Protestantism, as a movement, expected its women to be knowledgeable about the Bible and even fairly sophisticated points of doctrine.[30] These rising literacy rates correlate with the ideological winds blowing across the country at this time, which considered personal familiarity with the Scriptures essential. Hear the Word preached in church, read it among your families, meditate upon it in your private bed-chamber, memorize it and think about it if you cannot sit and read—such advice poured forth from countless sources. English Puritans, especially, exhibited a consuming hunger for sermons, sometimes attending several in one day, and what they could not travel to hear on Sunday, they would buy and read at home. While the established church's official position was that congregations should stay in their home parishes (and indeed, this was one point of contention between Puritans and bishops), printed sermons of Anglican divines also remained popular sellers into the eighteenth century.

The printing history of this era points to a widespread interest in all types of devotional literature, including books on doctrine, primers, prayer books, sermons, allegories and poetry, emblem books, spiritual biographies, bible commentaries, and meditation treatises. While it is not necessary to retrace ground which Helen White, John King, and others have covered, a glance at the statistics gives some indication of the cultural tidal wave this phenomenon became. C. John Sommerville has estimated that by 1640, approximately 630,000 Bibles and 800,000 psalters had been printed in England; by 1700, those totals reached approximately 1,290,000 Bibles and 1,770,000 psalters. These numbers, according to Sommerville, 'might well

---

29 Reynolds, 'Objection considered against the Duty of Singing,' in *Practical Discourses of Singing*, 143.

30 Evidenced by the lives (among others) of Lady Anne Southwell, Lady Fairfax, the Protestant martyrs Anne Askew and Lady Jane Grey, the Duchess of Suffolk, and Katherine Stubbes (see Philip Stubbes' *A Christal Glasse for Christian Women*). Margaret Patterson Hannay writes of this period, 'The number of copies sold of books specifically written for women indicates a substantial literacy rate,' *Silent But for the Word: Tudor Women as Patrons, Translators, and Writers of Religious Works*, Margaret Patterson Hannay, ed. (Kent University Press, 1985), 8. See also *The Private Life of an Elizabethan Lady: The Diary of Lady Margaret Hoby 1599-1605*, Joanna Moody, ed. (Phoenix Mill: Sutton Publishing Ltd., 1998); Jacqueline Eales, 'Samuel Clarke and the "Lives" of Godly Women in Seventeenth-Century England,' in W.J. Sheils and Diana Wood (eds.), *'Women in the Church' Studies in Church History*, 27 (1990); pp. 365-76; and Alison Wall, 'Elizabethan Precept and Feminine Practice: the Thynne Family of Longleat,' *History*, 75 (1990): pp. 23-7.

indicate a saturation of the literate population.'[31] Apart from these two books, fourteen other titles on religious subjects went through twenty or more editions (3,000 books per edition estimated) in the period from 1600 to 1711—in contrast, very few non-religious English titles reached even ten editions between 1600 and 1700. Michael Sparke's popular *Crumms of Comfort* underwent forty printings by 1652, and over sixty thousand copies were sold from his London shop near the Old Bailey.[32] Other devotional best-sellers such as John Rawlet's *The Christian monitor* and Richard Allestree's *The whole duty of man* were printed in such large quantities that one out of every ten English households during the period could have owned one. In short, religious titles comprised approximately 44 percent of all English publications in the years prior to 1640. Between 1660 and 1700, one-half of all books that underwent at least six editions were also religious in subject, as were two-thirds of those books with twelve editions or more.[33] These statistics equal, if not surpass, the distribution of best-sellers in the twentieth century. The popularity of religious subjects continued through the Restoration and into the early eighteenth century. Biblical criticism and sermons remained consistent favorites from 1660 to 1751, with 8,800 sermons published, averaging ninety-six separate titles a year.[34]

---

31 C. John Sommerville, 'On the Distribution of Religious and Occult Literature in Seventeenth Century England,' *The Library* 29 (1974): 223. Douglas Bush remarks: 'In Jaggard's *Catalogue* of 1619 nearly three-fourths of the books are religious and moral; in William London's *Catalogue of the Most Vendible books in England* (1657-1658) the space given to works of divinity equals that occupied by all other kinds together ... Grotius and Casaubon declared, in the middle of James' reign, that there was little or no literary scholarship in England, that theology was the only interest of educated men.' *English Literature in the Earlier Seventeenth Century*, 2nd ed. rev. (Oxford: Clarendon Press, 1962), 310; quoted in Joseph A. Galdon, *Typology and Seventeenth-Century Literature* (The Hague: Mouton, 1975), 12.

32 J. Sears McGee, *The Godly Man in Stuart England: Anglicans, Puritans, and the Two Tables, 1620-1670* (New Haven: Yale University Press, 1976), 25.

33 C. John Sommerville, *Popular Religion in Restoration England* (Gainesville: University of Florida Press, 1977), 30.

34 Thomas R. Preston, 'Biblical criticism, literature, and the eighteenth-century reader,' in *Books and their Readers in Eighteenth-Century England*, Isabel Rivers, ed. (Leicester: Leicester University Press, 1982), 97. Concerning the eighteenth century, Preston writes: 'There have been several studies of eighteenth-century reading habits and vogues, and all the evidence points to an almost astonishing interest in religious works generally and biblical criticism specifically ... as might be expected, sermons dominated religious publishing from the Restoration to the middle of the eighteenth century.' John Sommerville points out that 'While it is apparent that an indeterminate number of Englishmen existed at various removes from the culture represented by our books, there is evidence of widespread religious concern simply in the output of the religious press.' Sommerville, *Popular Religion*, 82.

Even before the reforms of Henry VIII, devotional literature had been available in England on a limited basis. Worthy of note were the primers, which derived from the medieval Book of Hours and contained prayers, Scripture, hymns, creeds, glosses, and colorful illustrations. Book of Hours in the vernacular had existed in manuscript form from the fourteenth century, and with the Reformation (and its attendant technological advances) a printed English primer became very popular, with over 180 editions appearing between 1525 and 1560.[35] But its popularity was superceded in time by the *Book of Common Prayer* (1549). Frequently bound together with the Geneva Bible and the metrical psalter, the BCP comprised part of a triumvirate which would have a profound impact upon the course of early English Protestantism. Also in the sixteenth century a different type of prayer-book appeared in print, represented by Thomas Becon's *Pomander of Prayer* and *The Flower of Godly Prayers* and Edward Dering's *Godly Private Praiers for Householders to meditate Upon, and to say in their Families.* Such collections featured meditations for readers from a variety of classes and stations in life: merchants, farmers, pregnant women, courtiers, children, and servants. Addressing the intimate and mundane concerns of English believers, these prayer-books exhibit the increasingly personal tone of the culture's collective piety.[36]

While it is impossible to do justice to such a wide-ranging genre in a few paragraphs, it should be noted that the moral life was frequently presented as an imaginative one as well. Protestant readers could decipher the fanciful symbolism in the popular emblem book by the royalist poet Francis Quarles. Herbert, Donne, Nahum Tate, George Wither, Nathaniel Ingelo, and Bishop Thomas Ken wrote sacred verse, some of it of outstanding quality. Men and women were exhorted to exercise their imaginations by 'reading the Providences,' pondering God's dealings with them in their own lives and through national and world events; and books such as Godfrey Goodman's *The Creatures Praysing God, or, the Religion of Dumb Creatures* modeled the kindred art of 'reading the Creatures,' the embracing of spiritual lessons through observation of the natural world— the timid hare, for example, might represent the timid soul: the raucous crow, the religious hypocrite—a favorite archetypal villain of the period.

The Word Sung

Paralleling this growing interest in devotional literature, the evidence suggests that English society during this era was taken with sacred vocal

---

35 Charles C. Butterworth, *The English primers, 1529-1545; their publication and connection with the English Bible and the Reformation in England* (Philadelphia: University of Pennsylvania Press, 1953), 1.

36 Helen C. White, *The Tudor Books of Private Devotion* (Madison: University of Wisconsin Press, 1951), 168.

music.[37] The first known printing of English 'moral and divine' songs ('song' referring to dialogues and part-songs as well as solo works) dates from the year 1530, when the anonymous *XX Songes*, an assortment of secular and religious pieces, appeared. This was the earliest known set of English part books of printed song in mensural notation—and it heralded the birth of a new and powerful domestic buying market.[38] Yet it is the story of the psalter, in particular, which indicates how deeply devotional song affected the nation's consciousness. Theologians from Augustine to Luther and Calvin held that the Psalms represent a miniature, or *summa*, of the entire Bible, and this idea of a distilled spiritual essence appealed strongly to the type of conscientious Christian the English Reformation engendered. Mass-produced psalters were easily incorporated into daily life: printed in the common tongue and conveniently small in size, they could be stored in a skirt or breech pocket for quick reference, and also carried to services.

The first printed English psalter on record is Myles Coverdale's *Goostly psalmes and spirituall songes* (*c.* 1538), intended to be a musical corollary to Coverdale's English translation of the Bible (1535). Clearly influenced by Lutheran hymnody, *Goostly psalmes* contains metrical psalms set to simple melodies, German and Latin hymns translated into English, and musical settings of the Ten Commandments, the *Magnificat*, and the *Pater Noster*. But the versifying efforts of Thomas Sternhold and John Hopkins[39] would in the end prove more enduring than Coverdale's: their *Whole Booke of Psalmes* (1562) quickly gained dominance, becoming the standard psalter throughout England, a pride of place it retained until Nahum Tate and Nicholas Brady's *A New Version* appeared in 1696 (indeed, the two versions co-existed for over a century after that; Sternhold and Hopkins would not be entirely supplanted as a popular favorite until the Regency period).[40] Its promise to be 'very meet to be used of all sorts of people privately for their solace and comfort,' clearly indicates the democratic nature of its audience. Published during what must have seemed the reassuringly Protestant climes of Elizabeth I, with the Marian exiles back in force and energetically pursuing their agenda of church reform, *The Whole Booke of Psalmes* held the promise of more to come, as over 600 complete

---

37 This study does not focus specifically upon devotional music which existed in manuscript form. See John Milsom, 'Sacred Songs in the Chamber,' in *English Choral Practice 1400-1650*, John Morehen, ed. (Cambridge: 1995), 168.

38 Peter Le Huray calls this publishing event 'the opening of the great era of Tudor and Stuart domestic music.' *Music and the Reformation in England 1549-1660*. (New York: Oxford University Press, 1967), 370.

39 As well as the Marian exiles Thomas Norton, William Whittingham, John Pullain, and William Kethe.

40 Nicholas Temperley, 'Psalms, metrical,' in *New Grove*.

editions of Sternhold and Hopkins would be printed in England over the next 270 years. Twenty different editions appeared between 1562 and 1579; forty-five between 1580 and 1599; sixty-five between 1600 and 1620, and over a hundred between 1620 and 1640.[41] With figures such as these, it is not surprising to learn that between 1562 and 1650 more psalters were printed in England than all other music books combined.[42]

The monophonic Sternhold and Hopkins was not the only musical version of the Psalms available in England. A harmonized version under the name *The whole psalmes in foure partes* appeared in 1563. Thomas East's *The Whole Booke of Psalmes* (1592) featured polyphonic settings by John Dowland, John Farmer, George Kirbye, and Giles Farnaby; it proved so popular that it underwent reprints in 1594, 1604, and 1611. In 1599, Richard Alison published *The Psalmes of David in Meter*, featuring his four-part arrangements and solo settings of selected Sternhold and Hopkins psalms with lute and bass viol accompaniment. Thomas Ravenscroft's *The Whole Booke of Psalmes* (1621) contained music by Ravenscroft, Thomas Tallis, Dowland, Thomas Morley, Farnaby, and John Bennet—like many other psalters of the time, Ravenscroft's collection includes original hymns as well as psalms. Later in the seventeenth century, John Playford published *Psalms and Hymns in Solemn Musick* (1671) for domestic use, followed in 1677 by his more comprehensive *The Whole Book of Psalms: with the usual Hymns and Spiritual Songs: together with all the ancient and proper Tunes sung in Churches, with some of later Use*. This collection, the last harmonized version of Sternhold and Hopkins, underwent nineteen editions and was popular well into the eighteenth century; Playford's son Henry later published a supplement to it entitled *The Divine Companion*.

Besides the psalters, other printed works contained sacred vocal music of varying degrees of musical sophistication. One early example is John Hall's *The Courte of Vertue* (1565), intended as a sacred parody of Thomas Wyatt's popular *The Courte of Venus*. Each chapter in *The Courte of Vertue* begins with a melody which accompanies that chapter's moralizing lyrics: Hall's original verses imitate the language of the Psalms, and the book also includes musical settings of the traditional *Nunc dimittis* and *Pater Noster*. In 1583 William Hunnis, a gentleman of the Chapel Royal, published the alliteratively-titled *Seven Sobs of a Sorrowfull Soule for Sinne*, containing his paraphrases of the seven penitential psalms set to melodies, as well as 'Comfortable Dialogues between Christ and a Sinner, touching the soul's health.' Among the most-renowned devotional pieces from the Elizabethan era are those of William Byrd, whose *Psalmes, sonnets, and songs of sadness and pietie* (1588), *Songs of sundrie natures* (1589), and *Psalmes,*

---

41 Le Huray, *Music and Reformation*, 376.
42 Peter Alan Munstedt, 'John Playford, Music Publisher: A Bibliographical Catalogue' (Ph.D. diss., University of Kentucky, 1983), 15.

songs, and sonnets (1611) intersperse secular songs with moral and
penitential themes. Besides Byrd, other English composers such as Thomas
Tomkins (*Songs*, 1622) and Francis Pilkington (*Second Set of Madrigals*,
1624) included devotional songs in their part-song collections. Several lute-
song books from the early seventeenth century also contained devotional
pieces, including John Bartlett's *A Booke of Ayres* (1606), Thomas
Campion's *Two Bookes of Ayres. The first contayning Divine and Morall
Songs* (1610), John Dowland's *A Pilgrimes Solace* (1612), and John Attey's
The First Booke of Ayres (1622). Other devotional song editions in the
seventeenth century include George Wither's *The Hymnes and Songs of the
Church* (1623), William Child's *First set of Psalmes of III Voyces* (1639),
Henry and William Lawes' *Choice Psalmes put into musick* (1648), Walter
Porter's *Mottets of Two Voyces* (1657), John Playford's *Cantica Sacra*
(1674), *Select Hymns Taken Out of Mr. Herbert's 'Temple'* (1697), Henry
Playford's *Harmonia Sacra* (in two volumes: 1688 and 1693) and *The
Divine Companion* (1701). These lists give strong indication of a culture
where singing flourished, and where a rigorous piety naturally formed the
air it breathed.

The psalms and devotional songs mentioned above were sung within a
variety of milieus, private, domestic, and public; and a consciousness of the
importance of these spheres of performance contributed to the growing
body of English thought surrounding the subject of singing. The Anglican
author Joseph Brookbank reveals a glimpse of the categorizing tendencies
of the early modern mind with his divisions of musical performance in *The
Well-tuned Organ*:

> 1. Private, and this two ways.
>   (1) Most private, when one sings with the voice, or plays on
>   musical Instruments solitarily, and by himself, to God, or himself,
>   or both.
>   (2) Less private, when singing, or playing on musical instruments
>   solitarily, and by himself, to God, or himself, or both.
>   2. Public: When either of these, or both, are used in a public
> assemblies, to God, or themselves, or both.[43]

Taking these definitions in reverse order, we shall first consider
devotional singing as it related to the public sphere. Worship services were
primary sites for the performance of sacred vocal music. As the majority of
English clergy—however they interpreted its practice—believed that
singing was mandated by scripture, participatory singing of some type
figured prominently in most English Protestant services from the sixteenth

---

43 Joseph Brookbank, *The Well-tuned Organ, or, an Exercitation: wherein, This
   Question is fully and largely discussed, Whether or no Instrumental, and Organical
   Musick be lawful in Holy Publick Assemblies?* (London, 1660), 3.

century onward (Quaker and some Baptist congregations excepted). Even in the days of Puritan ascendency during the civil war and the Commonwealth, when the traditional sung liturgy was disbanded, psalm-singing retained a position of honor in public assemblies.[44] Divines were acutely aware of the symbolism inherent within corporate singing, and prized it as a way to foster unity among the elect. In this way vocal music was believed to play an important emotional function as well as spiritual and instructional ones. William Harris claims that the

> Advantages of Singing ... extend to others as well as to our selves ... 'Tis mutually beneficial, and of extensive use. All concur together in this holy Exercise, and each one excites and assists the other. Every other Person, that sings the Praises of God, helps to excite the Affection, and raise the Devotion of my Soul; and my Singing helps to raise and excite another's. The Breath of Praise mutually fans one anothers' Souls, kindles a divine Heat, and blows it up into a Flame: and so every one contributes something to another's Good, and receives some help from every other.[45]

And as William Perkins explains in *A Cloud of Faithfull Witnesses*:

> Why do we sing [the Psalms] now in our churches? The answer is: The Church in all ages consists of a number of believers, and the faith is always one, and makes all that apprehend God's promises, to be alike to one another in grace, in meditations, in dispositions, in affection, in desires, in spiritual wants, in the feeling and use of afflictions, in course and conversation of life, and in performance of duties to God and man: and therefore the same Psalms, Prayers, and Meditations, are now as fit for the Church in these days, and are said and sung with the same use and profit.[46]

Writing in eighteenth-century Boston, Lemuel Hedge drew upon this same theological tradition when he observed:

> It adds much to the beauty of music, and makes it most melodious, to have the united voices of a multitude, harmonizing together in song. God

---

44 Some have speculated that Cromwell's restrictions on certain types of public music during the Commonwealth actually encouraged the habit of domestic musical performance (in which vocal music was prominent). While puritan censorship is historical fact, to dismiss seventeenth-century Puritanism entirely as an anti-musical ideology is simplistic and shuts us off from understanding an important movement in English and colonial history. The most complete work on this subject remains Percy Scholes' *The Puritans and Music in England and New England* (London: Oxford University Press, 1934).

45 William Harris, 'The Excellence of the Duty of Singing,' in *Practical Discourses of Singing*, 79.

46 William Perkins, *A Cloud of Faithfull Witnesses, Leading To The Heavenly Canaan: Or, A Commentarie upon the eleventh Chapter to the Hebrewes* (London, 1622), 76.

has made men, as well as angels, sociable creatures, and he expects and requires that they unite together in offering up their praises to Him: And as it is good for them to dwell, so to sing together in unity.[47]

Along similar lines was William Ames's reply to the question *What use hath Singing above the ordinary pronunciation?*—'It hath more command of mutual edification, if it be with others.'[48] Certainly Christian unity was an ideal which must have been difficult to maintain on a local level, let alone a national one. Not only was there a tendency towards partisan bickering, but differences in life experience, class, age, and sex could also hinder feelings of mutual communion. Nonconformist, Independent, and Baptist meetings attracted worshippers from a variety of social classes, resulting in a mix which could very well tax the spirit of Christian love. Even the Anglican parish system grouped together people who might not have freely associated with each other; plus, there was always the cross to bear of neighbors who were not as hygienic or fastidious as oneself. In the act of singing, at least, worshippers could raise their voices together and be assured that they indeed belonged to the invisible Church Universal.

Singing figured prominently in the English conception of domestic life as well. 'Every well-minded family by singing can make themselves a little church. And every church make themselves a little Heaven,' claimed Nathaniel Homes.[49] Since several generations of family-members, as well as servants and apprentices, often lived under one roof, households of the time could be quite large in contrast to the modern family; nevertheless, the home represented a curtailed social sphere, the 'less private' of Brookbank's performance categories. Singing played an important function within this dynamic as it joined with family prayers, catechizing, and oral reading of religious literature to create a type of domestic parallel to the public church service. The historian Christopher Hill has called this social phenomenon which swept across England 'the spiritualization of the household.'[50] The growing regard for the domestic sphere was nourished by deep theological roots, for, alongside its individualistic emphasis on the inner life, Reformation doctrine had always stressed the importance of family worship. Both Luther and Calvin advocated this type of familial worship outside of the church—*hausliche andacht, exercice spirituelle*—and the English Protestant home, in turn, came to be revered as a type of

---

47 Lemuel Hedge, *The duty and manner of singing in Christian churches* (Boston, 1772), 18.

48 Ames, *Conscience with the power and causes thereof*, 43.

49 Nathaniel Homes, *Gospel Musick. Or, the Singing of Davids Psalms, &c. In the public Congregations, or private Families asserted, and vindicated* (London, 1644), 12.

50 Christopher Hill, *Society and Puritanism in Pre-Revolutionary England* (London: Seeker and Warburg, 1964), chap. 13.

'little church,' the necessary foundation of a godly society. Indeed, it was to the household that much of the era's literary and artistic energies were directed. Richard Baxter indicates as much (and incidentally reveals something of his regard for the power of the voice) when he writes:

> The Writings of Divines are nothing else but a preaching the Gospel to the eye, as the voice preacheth it to the ear. Vocal preaching hath the preeminence in moving the affections, and being diversified according to the state of the Congregations which attend it: This way the Milk cometh warmest from the breast. But Books have the advantage in many other respects: you may read an able Preacher when you have but a mean one to hear. Every Congregation cannot hear the most judicious or powerful Preachers; but every single person may read the Books of the most powerful and Judicious; Preachers may be silenced or banished, when Books may be at hand … If Sermons be forgotten, they are gone. But a Book we may read over and over till we remember it: and if we forget it, may again peruse it at our pleasure, or at our leisure … *Books are (if well chosen) domestic, present, constant, judicious, pertinent, yea, and powerful Sermons.* [emphasis added][51]

Given this interest in domestic affairs, a number of books of practical divinity appeared in the sixteenth and seventeenth centuries which addressed the specific situations of English families. Singing figures prominently in these writings: Richard Bernard's *Iosuah's Godly Resolution … touching household governement for well ordering a familie* lists it among recommended devotional exercises: 'Reading of the holy Scriptures, the voice of God, Catechising, telling some short story of some notable example of the word, making use thereof, singing of psalms, and when the public sermon hath been heard, to repeat thereof as much as is remembered.'[52] *The Accomplished Singer* encourages in a similar vein,

> As no Persons are to be exempted, so no Places are to be excluded from the Reasonable Service; but we are to Sing everywhere, Lifting up an Holy voice, unto the Lord. Not only should we with all our Heart Praise the Eternal God, where the Upright meet Privately, and where more Publicly; But also the Christian Householder should make this one of his Daily Sacrifices … the Faithful in the Primitive Times, had the Psalms by heart, so that they would Recreate themselves with Singing them in the Streets and in the Fields, as well as in their Dwellings.[53]

Baxter's *Christian Directory* also suggests that families adopt a rigorous schedule of singing, catechizing, and prayer, to be observed twice a day

---

51 Richard Baxter, *A Christian Directory* (London, 1673), 60.

52 Richard Bernard, *Iosuah's Godly Resolution in conference with Caleb, touching household governement for well-ordering a familie* (London, 1612), 27.

53 Mather, *Accomplished Singer*, 21.

during the week, and several times on Sunday. Nor was devotional singing limited to families with Puritan leanings: while Anglican households were typically less extemporaneous, preferring to follow the liturgies contained within the BCP, popular accounts indicate that they enjoyed performing 'divine and moral songs' as well. Especially remarkable in this regard was Nicholas Ferrar's Anglican community at Little Gidding in Huntingdonshire. Ferrar—theologian, friend to George Herbert, and a man of ecumenical religious tastes—carefully created an artistic and intellectual environment where family, friends, and visitors observed a type of rarefied Protestant monasticism, and singing punctuated the traditional Christian hours. While it would be misleading to present Little Gidding as normative of the average English household during this era, Ferrar's experiment remains an idealized example of how far the culture's impulse toward domestic piety could extend, given the right circumstances.[54]

The Personalized Voice

These authors witness to early English Protestantism's real and often solicitous interest in matters of public and domestic life; yet, as an ideological movement it is best known for its emphasis upon the personal application of religious truths.[55] 'A godly man can make a good use of Privacy,' exclaims Richard Sibbes in *The Soules Conflict with it Selfe*. Unlike the unbeliever, 'who cannot endure solitariness, because his heart is empty,' the Christian welcomes and seek out opportunities for reading the 'book of the heart,' for 'by this means we shall never want a Divine to comfort us, a physician to cure us, a Counsellor to direct us, a Musician to cheer us, a Controller to check us, because (by help of the word and Spirit) we can be all these to our selves.'[56] With this advice in mind, Brookbank's definition of 'most private' music gains new immediacy: a solitary man, woman, or child sings or plays a musical instrument 'to himself, to God, or to both.' Diaries and biographies from the period frequently allude to the habit of private singing for solace and comfort; and singing alone, early in the morning or late at night, perhaps in one's bedchamber, perhaps accompanied by lightly plucking a lute or softly pressing the keys of a virginal, was a type of performance which allowed for an especially

---

54 See Bernard Blackstone, ed., *The Ferrar Papers, Containing a Life of Nicholas Ferrar; the Winding-Sheet, an Ascetic Dialogue; a Collection of Short Moral Histories; a Selection of Family Letters*, (Cambridge: Cambridge University Press, 1938).

55 While Puritanism was the branch of early English Protestantism most associated with a penchant for self-examination, Anglicans such as Joseph Hall and Ussher were equally concerned with it.

56 Richard Sibbes, *The Soules Conflict with it Selfe: and victory over it Self by Faith* (London, 1635), 60.

intimate embrace of the transcendent message. As one nonconformist divine put it, 'The Voice of Praise will sweeten Retirement, perfume the closet, and bring down the best of Company to us or carry up our Souls to that which is so: This has been found, by many a poor Sufferer, a strong Consolation in their dark and solitary Dungeons and Prisons.'[57] Secular writings also discussed private music making. Roger North, in his memoir *The Musicall Grammarian*, places it first in his categories of performance, as does Brookbank. North's comments are revealing, for while we recognize his first point, that private music is an opportunity to gain technical dexterity, we have forgotten his second point, that it has possible moral benefits as well. '[Solitary music] is a medicine without any nausea or bitter and is taken both for pleasure and cure ... the moral consequence is enough to recommend it, as a means of diverting other ways of consuming spare time more pernicious, than this is pleasing.'[58]

Both quiet solitude and family life provided congenial environments for 'applying the word' through music. Within the early English Protestant devotional culture, the voice came to represent a primary vehicle for spiritual transformation. Believers could, through singing, identify with biblical characters, learn vicariously from their struggles, and gain comfort and reassurance. This significance is due in large part to the close association between the human voice and the book of Psalms. Interest in psalmody cut across all classes during this era: while Philip Sidney's *The Psalmes of David in Metre* established a standard of polished elegancy in the late sixteenth century which other poets strove to emulate, English society at-large embraced the stolid rhythms of Sternhold and Hopkins.[59] Being poetic expressions of the Word, the Psalms were imbued with all of the supernatural virtues and powers inherent in that concept. Early English Protestantism inherited a formidable body of Christian writings on this subject, and revived many of the themes contained in these earlier sources. Patristic theologians had singled out the Psalms for their intuitive insight into the human condition. St. Basil proclaimed:

All Scripture is inspired by God and is useful ... but, the Book of Psalms has taken over what is profitable from all. It foretells coming events; it

---

57 Benjamin Gravener, 'An Exhortation to the Duty of Singing,' in *Practical Discourses of Singing*, 217.

58 Roger North, *The Musicall Grammarian* (London, 1728), 197.

59 Hallett Smith notes four historical motivations for the sixteenth-century vogue of versifying the Psalms: 1) the knowledge that the originals were poetry, 2) better ease of memorization, 3) to provide a spiritual equivalent to secular poetry, and 4) for use as a personal devotional exercise. He writes, 'The vogue was not limited, in the middle years of the century, to any religious group or to any literary school or to any level of poetical talent.' 'English Metrical Psalms in the Sixteenth Century and their Literary Significance,' *Huntington Library Quarterly* 9 (February 1946), 268.

recalls history; it frames laws for life; it suggest what must be done; and in general, it is the common treasury of good doctrine carefully finding what is suitable for each one. The old wounds of souls it cures completely, and to the recently wounded it brings speedy improvement; the diseased it treats, and the unharmed it preserves. On the whole, it effaces, as far as possible, the passions, which subtly exercise dominion over such souls during the lifetime of man, and it does this with a certain orderly persuasion and sweetness which produces sound thoughts.[60]

Martin Luther wrote centuries later:

Wherever the feelings of joy are described, you will never find the sensations of a heart, filled with gladness and exultation, more significantly and expressively described, than in the Psalms of thanksgiving, or the Psalms of praise ... On the other hand, you will never find the straits, the sorrows, and the pains of a distressed mind any where described in a more expressive manner than in the Psalms of temptation, or of complaints; as in Psalm vi. and the like; where you see all dark and gloomy, all full of anguish and distress, under a sight and sense of divine wrath, and the working of despair.

And so again, where the Psalms are speaking of hope or fear, they so describe those feelings in their true and native colours, that no Demosthenes or Cicero could ever equal them in liveliness, or descriptiveness of expression. For, as I have before observed, the Psalms have this peculiarity of excellence above all other books of description ... this that above all things gives a seriousness, and reality to the feelings— it is this that affects, as it were, the very bones and the marrow—when a creature feels itself speaking in the very sight and presence of its God![61]

And Calvin explained:

Not without cause am I wont to term this book the Anatomy of all the parts of the Soul, inasmuch as a man shall not find any affection in himself, whereof the Image appeareth not in the glass. Yea rather, the holy Ghost hath here lively set out before our eyes, all the griefs, sorrows, fears, doubts, hopes, cares, anguishes, and finally all the troublesome motions wherewith men's minds are wont to be turmoiled.[62]

---

60 St. Basil, *Exegetic Homilies*, Agnes Clare Way, tr. (Washington, D.C.: Church Fathers, 1963), 151-154; quoted in Eugene Robert Cunnar, 'Richard Crashaw and the Hymn Tradition: Seventeenth-Century Lord of the Lyre' (Ph.D. diss., University of Chicago, 1973), 86.

61 Quoted in Barbara Kiefer Lewalski, *Protestant Poetics and the Seventeenth-Century Religious Lyric* (Princeton: Princeton University Press), 44.

62 Quoted in ibid., 43.

Similar tributes are scattered liberally throughout early modern English sources. The sixteenth-century divine Thomas Becon writes that the poet David

> comforteth the comfortless. He exhorteth the sinner unto amendment of life. He lifteth up the desperate unto the hope of God's mercy … He healeth the diseased. He raiseth up the dead unto life. He maketh the sad merry. He exhilarateth and rejoiceth the merrily disposed. To conclude, he is a Minstrel fit for all kind of persons, so that they be bent unto godliness.[63]

They all shared the belief that the Psalms are divinely-inspired and thus singularly relevant—*useful*, wrote Basil—to God's people throughout the ages. The emotions expressed through the Psalms were believed to represent the entire spectrum of human feeling, from deepest despair to hope and joy. Luther writes that the workings of the inner psyche are 'more significantly and expressively described' in the Psalms than anywhere else, exceeding even the classics. In wake of this attitude, many English psalters recommended specific Psalms to match personal conditions. An index to *The Whole Booke of Psalmes* (1567) suggests:

> If thine acquaintance persecute thee, and many rise against thee, thou hast the third Psalm … If thou feelest the threatenings of God, and thereby perceivest thy self to be dismayed, thou mayst say the 6. Psalm, and the 37. Psalm … If thou seest the wicked prosper in peace, be not so offended that thou be moved, but say the 73. Psalm … If thou be thrust into a college, or into a parish, town, or country, whose inhabitors are wicked, crafty, and malicious pick-quarrels, wouldest be delivered from them, use the 120. Psalm.[64]

Similarly, Ravenscroft's *The Whole Booke of Psalmes: with the Hymnes Evangelicall, and Songs Spirituall* (1621) offers appropriate Psalms to sing when one feels contrite, thankful, forsaken, dejected, happy, or 'finds life tedious.'

This preference for an increasingly personalized brand of devotion is also apparent in populist prayer books which began appearing in the mid-sixteenth century. Thomas Becon's *Pomander of Prayer* and *The Flower of Godly Prayers* contain prayers for people from all walks of life: fathers, mothers, children, servants, magistrates, gentlemen, laborers, and the destitute. His prayers address concerns accompanying each state: the prayer for a pregnant woman asks God for a safe delivery for mother and child, while the prayer for a single man petitions for help in avoiding sexual temptation. In the same way, the popular Geneva Bible also gave the

---

63 Quoted in Hallet Smith, 'English Metrical Psalms,' 259.
64 Quoted in White, *Tudor Books of Private Devotion*, 44.

impression of a universal yet intensely personal faith by identifying the struggles of its readers with the lives of biblical characters.[65] Its title-page woodcut depicts the Israelites safely crossing the Red Sea with the Egyptians in hot pursuit, with captions from Ex.14:13 and 14: 'Fear ye not, stand still, and behold the salvation of the Lord, which he will show to you this day. The Lord shall fight for you: therefore hold you your peace'; and Ps. 34:19: 'Great are the troubles of the righteous but the Lord delivereth them out of all.' The message for English Protestants, beleaguered on all sides by the threat of Catholic Europe, was clear: 'The Lord will surely fight for *you*, in your own time: your troubles may seem insurmountable, but take these ancient lessons to heart, and rest assured that God is on your side today.' The analogy between Protestant Britain and ancient Israel became a theological and literary commonplace. Isaac Watts commonly interchanged the two in his psalm paraphrases for congregational singing: '*O Britain*, trust the Lord: Thy foes in vain/Attempt thy ruin, and oppose his reign.' And the scholar Ruth Smith makes a compelling case for this tradition's influence upon both the creation and reception of Handel's oratorio librettos.[66]

All of these exercises in devotional empathy were practical expressions of the typological interpretative mode in theology, a way of thinking which played a formative role in early English Protestant belief. Medieval scholastics had traditionally recognized four distinct senses of Scripture: the literal, allegorical, moral (or tropological), and anagogical. Theologians allied with the Reformation, on the other hand, while acknowledging the validity of the four modes, tended to emphasize the literal above others; many of Protestantism's historical distinctives correspondingly stem from this divergence in interpretative styles. While literalism is a habit of mind easily scorned, the early reformers believed that by calling for a return to the literal mode they were clearing away a confusing tangle of allegory which had, over the centuries, grown up and obscured the simple message of salvation. And doesn't every man, woman, and child in England (they would argue) deserve to hear the gospel, in all its plain beauty? William Tyndale exemplifies this attitude in *The Obedience of a Christian Man* (1528), where he criticizes the Roman church for having reduced the literal sense of Scripture to 'nothing at all,' and accuses the pope of locking it up 'with the false and counterfeited keys of his traditions, ceremonies, and feigned lies.'[67]

---

65 Undergoing 140 editions after its initial appearance in 1560, the Geneva Bible rivalled the Authorized Version in popularity among English Protestants through the seventeenth century.

66 See Ruth Smith, *Handel's Oratorios*.

67 William Tyndale, *Doctrinal Treatises and Introduction to Different Portions of the Holy Scriptures by William Tyndale, Martyr, 1536*, H. Walter, ed., 303; quoted in Ira

This trait of emphasizing the literal meaning of Scripture went hand-in-hand with a preoccupation with typology, a school of biblical exegesis which interprets the Old Testament as both historical account and symbolic foreshadowing of the New Testament. Within this scheme, for example, the original Adam, while having been an actual person, at the same time prefigures the second Adam, Christ; the story of the Jews crossing the Red Sea points toward Christian baptism; the paschal lamb represents Christ's blood-stained sacrifice; and the land of Canaan symbolizes the kingdom of heaven. The Old Testament reality is the type, and its fulfilment in the New Testament, the antitype. Differing from symbol (which transcends literal meaning to indicate some abstraction) and allegory (a series of metaphors relaying one central message), typology points instead to an analogous historical or personal fulfilment, a 'specific parallel between two historical entities.'[68] Through this kind of exegesis, Anglican and Puritan divines believed that they were revealing a unity in Scripture which confirms the constancy and faithfulness of God: just as God had fulfilled his purposes in the biblical dispensation, his hand was at work in England as well. Many Protestants came to believe, sometimes quite fervently, that within their own lives they were, in a sense, 'post-figuring' biblical events and characters.[69] Contemplating one's past remained a prominent feature of

---

Clark, *Christ Revealed: The History of the Neotypological Lyric in the English Renaissance* (Gainesville: University Press of Florida, 1982), 11.

68 G.R. Osborne, 'Typology,' *Evangelical Dictionary of Theology*, Walter A. Elwell, ed. (Grand Rapids: Baker Book House, 1984), 1118.

69 I am indebted to Murray Roston for my use of the term 'post-figuring:' Here he uses it to describe the empathy Protestants felt with characters in sixteenth-century religious dramas: 'The Protestant's growing concern with the Covenant tradition gave the Old Testament stories a new archetypal significance. For if the covenant reaffirmed throughout the generations was contracted with the individual as well as the group, then the Protestant's own life should bear the marks of that cyclical repetition. As he read the biblical tales of the patriarchs, prophets, and kings, and of their struggle for moral probity in the midst of worldly temptation, the Protestant looked for their true meaning in his own spiritual and even political exertions. He began to see himself in biblical terms, re-enacting or 'post-figuring' in his life leading incidents from the lives of the scriptural heroes. Instead of searching in the Old Testament for stories whose validity lay in their adumbrating the New, he now searched for those which seem to parallel his own personal history, those which he felt were being relived by him in a later generation. Sometimes, it is true, the saints had been seen retrospectively as having re-enacted the Passion of Christ and fulfilled in their deaths the requirement of *imitatio Dei.* But here was an essentially new concept, with its roots in the soil of the temporal world, whereby mortal men, not elevated into sainthood, began to see their daily struggles, both spiritual and physical, in terms of a biblical archetype ... and implicit in this postfiguration was the encouraging conviction that the victorious destiny of the biblical hero was, by

early English Protestant meditation, for it was thought that 'past troubles do season, and as it were ballast present comforts, as the Snow in Winter increaseth the beauty of the Spring.' Also, believers could learn from the experiences of others.[70]

In his book *Christ Revealed: The History of the Neotypological Lyric in the English Renaissance*, Ira Clark relates this theological paradigm to period literature. He notes that much English Renaissance poetry can be termed 'neotypological' in that it utilizes typological imagery, and that devotional poets seeped in this tradition even applied biblical typology to their role in the creative process. He further suggests that Reformed typology encouraged the development of 'a distinctive kind of lyric persona,' an intermediary *neotype*, defined as 'contemporary people in the predicaments of types [i.e., facing similar situations as biblical characters], fully realizing in humility that Christ, the exalted antitype, redeems them.'[71] In contrast to medieval and counter-reformation *imitatio Dei* tradition, the neotype does not presume to try to imitate Christ *directly*; rather, it embodies within itself 'the individuality and failure of a type, and thereby realize[s] salvation through Christ, the antitype.' In this way the English Renaissance poet 'would be releasing and exploiting the tremendous expressive potential latent in types.'[72] For, according to Clark, the Old Testament type, 'real and valuable in its own right,' also represented to the culture a 'failure inside time [i.e., fallible humanity in a fallen world],' which it recognized could only be fulfilled and perfected by the New Testament antitype. The neotype is thus an intricate configuration, simultaneously connecting the type and antitype, the past and the future, and also linked to the eternal Christ. Clark believes that this tension accounts for much of the psychologically complex nature of English metaphysical poetry:

A Reformed persona fails to recognize his salvation because he sees himself in a constricted Old Testament context. Meanwhile the poem is establishing the persona's reformation by alluding to the New Testament antitype. The persona is thereby contrite and exalted at the same time. Thus, these lyricists could devoutly sing of God entering actual people, things, and events in their own time, and of his entering into neotypes, out

---

virtue of the other parallels, the destiny of the postfigurer too; so that Milton in his spiritual darkness found some comfort in the belief that his salvation must lie before him.' Murray Roston, *Biblical Drama in England* (Evanston: Northwestern University Press, 1965), 70.

70 Edward Reynoldes, *A Treatise of the Passions and Faculties of the Soul of Man* (London, 1647), 205.

71 Clark, *Christ Revealed*, 4.

72 Ibid., 21.

of their faith that he has entered time through Old Testament types and through the saving and perfecting New Testament antitype, Christ.[73]

Clark continues on to remark that, through applying biblical characters and emotions in this personal way, early English Protestants (1) perceived their lives as being cosmically significant, (2) vicariously experienced personal failure and repentence, and (3) through forgiveness, believed that they participated (albeit incompletely) in the divine glories of Christ and heaven. Put simply, they 'were essentially placing themselves at the core of a saving interaction between God's eternal transcendence and history's mundane limits.'[74]

Building upon this idea, I propose that the human voice in early modern England became a uniquely personal representation of the intermediating neotype, as the voice was perceived as an expression grounded in the body, yet ultimately transcendent by virtue of the supernatural power of the word. In hearing the stories of great heroes from the Bible, in effect re-living the struggles of an earlier epoch, believers would feel a great need for some type of self-expression, a way to participate more directly in this salvation drama, both in and out of the public worship service. Singing aptly contributes the appropriate personal aspect in this dynamic. I believe that this symbolic function of the voice was not lost to men and women in early modern England. Just as no two snowflakes are alike, each voice is distinct, a fact made increasingly clear by recent technological innovations in voice-print identification. The voice transmits a great deal of information about the individual: sex, age, condition of health, regional origin, personality, and emotional state. It is also immediately recognizable—to other people, and, most importantly, to the Creator of that voice. 'Hear my cry, oh Lord,' the Psalms plead repeatedly; and few in the devotional culture of the time doubted that God knew the individual soul behind each voice, very well indeed.

Singing thus conveyed a very real sense that believers were actively participating in the world of universal Christian archetypes. In line with their pastoral orientation, early modern divines described how this type of psychological transferral was to take place. Believers were to attempt to imagine and thus re-create within themselves the emotional states of the inspired authors: a type of pre-Stanislavskian method acting technique, if you will. William Ames asked a question which was on many Protestants' minds at this time: 'How are we to sing those historic Psalms which belong to other persons and times?' In other words, what should a singer's demeanor and attitude be, how can he or she actually take on this biblical persona? His answer: 'We ought in our thoughts to put on, as it were, the

---

73 Ibid., 5.
74 Ibid., 28.

person, either of them, of whom those Psalms were composed, or of them who composed them, that whatever is spoken there, we may, in some sort, take it as spoken to ourselves.'[75] Along similar lines, Cotton Mather in *The Accomplished Singer* describes how the writers of the Psalms, through the inspiration of the Holy Spirit, first experienced 'those Motions of Piety, which were agreeable and answerable to the Matter then flowing from their Pens'; he subsequently advises Christians to 'study and Labour for such Impressions of Piety on our Minds, as we may easily discover to have been upon the Minds of the Inspired Writers, at the Time when they wrote the spiritual songs, which we are now singing unto the Lord.'[76] He goes on to say that something about the act of singing itself has a unique power to re-create these archetypal emotions:

> In Singing our spiritual songs, let us be Inquisitive after those Motions of piety, which are discernible in the Verse now before us; and let us with a Soul flying away to God, for them, try whether we cannot fly with them; and strive to come at the like; and give not over the struggle, till we feel our selves come into an holy Symphony with the Saints who had their Hearts burning within them, when they Sang these things unto the Lord.

He further indicates that this struggle to achieve emotional empathy, if successful, might even raise the passions to a level of spiritual ecstasy.

> Christian, Behold a lovely Method of getting into those heavenly Frames and Strains which will assure thee of thy arriving one Day, to the same state of Blessedness, and those Everlasting Habitations, which these Favourites and Amanuenses of Heaven, thro' whom our spiritual songs were convey'd unto us, have been renew'd into. Yea, Thou art already Caught up to Paradise in them. Nor is there a Nobler Method, among all our Hermeneutic Instruments, to come at the True sense of our spiritual songs, than ... an experimental Taste, of the piety which was working in the Hearts of the Writers at the Time of their Inspiration. Even an Illiterate Christian, that Lives unto God, and is no Stranger to the Sentiments of Piety, may in that way reach the true sense of the lively Oracles, and ... he will have within him, an exposition far more Valuable, than any of the Commentators ... who are Alienated from the Life of God, can help him to.[77]

Given orthodox Protestantism's high view of scripture, this is a remarkable statement by Mather, for he claims that modern-day singers can experience emotions of piety *identical* to those which inspired the original writers of the Psalms, thereby gaining that experimental 'taste' of holiness

75 Ames, *Conscience*, 44.
76 Mather, *Accomplished Singer*, 12.
77 Ibid.

which teaches and transforms the soul. A few pages later he suggests that, through singing, one can even begin to know the feelings of Jesus himself:

> O Believer, Sing the Graces, the Actions, the Sufferings and the Grandeurs of thy Incomparable Saviour; *Yea, get as far as thou canst into the Sentiments*, that may somewhat resemble those, which the Prophetic Spirit here assigns unto thy Saviour, in the Time of His Working out thy Salvation for thee. [emphasis added][78]

In a similar vein, Mather considers the question of how one should perform the imprecatory psalms, those which express anger and a desire for vengeance against God's enemies. What type of inner graces can one cultivate while mouthing such distinctly uncharitable sentiments? Mather replies that singers in this case should direct their feelings of hatred more abstractly against their own sins and lusts, or towards the devil, *not* towards other people.[79]

This interest in singing's power to re-create inner psychological states was linked to an emphasis upon personal sincerity in performance and the idea that one's heart and life must be in tune with the words coming out of one's mouth. While we find similar advice dating back to Augustine, this devotional literature as a whole, replete as it is with warnings against the wiles of religious hypocrites, gives the feeling of a culture particularly sensitive to the sins of dissemblance. Singers were urged to pay close attention at all times to the meaning of the lyrics and thereby 'attend to the matter as well as the manner of the song.'[80] English Reformers liked to quote Carthusianus: *'Dirige Cor sursum; profer bene; respice sensum.'*/ 'Direct your heart upwards; Offer a prayer well; Look to the meaning.' Integrity in singing was considered so important that neglecting it was done at one's own peril. Calvin warned that singing the Psalms with anything

---

78 Ibid., 19.
79 Writing on *personas*, James Anderson Winn calls the concept that 'poetry and music should express the actual emotions of their makers' a literary and musical development of the eighteenth century, which he juxtaposes against an earlier 'essentially imitative and rhetorical aesthetic.' He finds it revolutionary that Johann Mattheson in *Der Vollkommene Capellmeister* (1739) 'advocates that a composer assume a persona, imagine a 'subtext,' sink himself into a passion in order to express it.' While Mather's *The Accomplished Singer* also appeared in the early eighteenth century (1721), it derived its ideas on psychological empathy from the older English Protestant fascination with 'heart-sincerity,' rather than new intellectual trends from Continental musical treatises. Perhaps the theological sub-text explored here contributed in some part to the paradigm shift Winn is describing, which he does acknowledge is 'a result of many factors.' See Winn, *Unsuspected Eloquence: A History of the Relations between Poetry and Music* (Yale University Press, 1981), especially 194-199 and 232-238 *passim*, 'The *Affektenlehre* and the *Persona*.'
80 Hedge, *Duty and Manner*, 36.

less than total sincerity in the heart actually provokes the wrath of God.[81]
The nonconformist minister Earl Jabez cautioned, 'Let us think with our
selves, that while are conscientiously singing the Praises of God in his
Church below, we are training up for that better World ... and not forget to
consider what a dreadful thing it will be, to have our Cries and Wailings in
Hell receive a higher accent from our Hypocritical Songs of Praise on
Earth.' Singing holy songs thus represented a serious undertaking, one
which required concentration, self-vigilance, and, above all, a tender and
pliable heart—for 'Sighs are the figures that move Almighty God, and tears
the fluent and most current Rhetoric before him.'[82]

Three Examples from the Literature: Hall, Wither, and Bunyan

Three works from successive generations concretely illustrate the
empathetic function the singing voice came to adopt within the English
devotional culture during this era. Beginning with the sixteenth century,
John Hall's song collection entitled *The Courte of Vertue* was published in
1565 as a religious parody of a popular anthology of Petrarchan love songs
entitled *The Court of Venus*. Hall was a true Renaissance man whose
scholarly interests included medicine, poetry, and psalm translation
(*Certayne Chapters taken out of the Proverbes of Solomon, with Chapters
of the Holy Scripture, and certayne psalmes of David, translated into
English Metre*, 1549).[83] Each chapter of *The Courte of Vertue* begins with a
melody which accompanies that chapter's verses: both the style and content
of the original lyrics are heavily influenced by the Psalms, and the book
also contains music for traditional Latin hymns such as *Nunc dimittis* and
the *Pater Noster*.

What is most interesting about this volume is how it identifies, like the
psalters, the subjective moods and emotions of its public, and then offers
therapeutic relief through singing. The indexed topics in *The Courte of
Vertue* span a wide range of subjects, from health to character. Titles
include:

Against envy	Friendship
Against wrath	Gluttony
Arrogancy in students	Reverence to age

---

81 Calvin, *Institutes* 3.20.31.

82 Daniel Featley, *Ancilla Pietatis: or, the Hand-Maid to private Devotion: presenting
a Manuall to her Mistresse, furnished with Instructions, Hymns and Prayers*
(London, 1647), 132.

83 John Hall later published *The Proverbes of Salamon, three chapters of Ecclesiastes,
the sixthe chapter of Sapientia, the ix chapter of Ecclesiasticus, and certayne
psalmes of David* (London, n.d.), apparently in part to correct the presumption that
some of his earlier Proverbs translations were by Thomas Sternhold.

| Be not over thy wife jealous | Slanderous tongues |
| False weights and measures | Graces at meals |

While only a footnote in musical history, *The Courte of Vertue* does represent a milestone of sorts, for it clearly lays out the three pillars of the empathy dynamic under discussion: devotional lyrics, the singing voice, and the psychological and spiritual condition of the audience.

Decades later, when civil war loomed on the English horizon, a work reminiscent of *The Courte of Vertue,* but much larger in scope, appeared: George Wither's *Haleluiah, or, Britain's Second Remembrancer* (1641). Like Hall, Wither was a man of wide-ranging interests—he was, at various times, a lawyer, writer, poet, and officer in Cromwell's New Model army. The story of Wither's religious allegiances is a good example of the shifting boundaries between mainstream Anglican and Puritan during this century: while the liturgicalism of *Hymnes and Songs of the Church* (1623) displays Wither's early establishment Anglicanism, his military service two decades later leaves no doubt as to his eventual identification with the more radical Puritanism. Wither had a special fascination with sacred music and poetry throughout his life. When *Hymnes* and *Songs of the Church* first appeared with music by Orlando Gibbons, it was intended to be bound into pew psalters and become an official musical supplement for Anglican services. This project fell through, to Wither's regret, and England would have to wait for John Mason, Benjamin Keach, and Isaac Watts for a native school of hymn-writing to come into its own.

In physical size alone, *Haleluiah* is a daunting work. It contains no notation, yet its intent is clearly musical. Wither suggests popular psalm and hymn tunes to match his verses ('Sing this as the *Magnificat* ... the *Pater-noster*'). He also refers to secular tunes ('Sing this, as *I loved once*'). The 273 hymns in *Haleluiah* address a broad array of personal concerns, as Wither attempts a complete musical guide to the totality of human experience. The first section, 'Hymns Occasional,' contains such titles as 'When we first awake,' 'When we put on our Apparel,' 'A Hymn whilst we are washing,' 'When we are at our Labour,' 'When we return Home,' and 'In a clear Starry Night.' In case of insomnia, there is 'When we cannot sleep.' Meditations upon a variety of activities include: 'When we ride for Pleasure,' 'When we are upon the Seas,' 'When we are Walking in a Garden,' and 'For a Sheep-shearing.' Some seem humorous: 'A Lamentation in times of excessive Rain.' Wither cites the unifying power of singing in preface to the hymn 'When kindred meet together':

The love of kindred is grown cold; and many unkindnesses and neglects are among them. Therefore, when they visit each other, this Hymn being sung, may remember them, to cherish that Amity which ought to be between them.

Reconciliation achieved, this is followed by the sentimental 'When Kindred depart from each other.'

Wither includes the rather quirky title, 'A Hymn encouraging sick persons to be willing to die.' While mutability and *ars moriendi* themes were traditional song subjects for centuries, this song addresses the obvious problem of how a dying person can marshal the physical stamina to perform such reveries. Acknowledging that 'Sick persons are not usually disposed to sing,' Wither reasons 'yet some are sometimes desirous to cheer up their hearts, and strengthen themselves against the fears of Death, by considering the Privileges of Life-eternal,' then concedes: 'perhaps they who want strength to sing this Hymn, shall receive comfort to hear these Meditations sung by others in their presence.'[84] The dying lips whisper:

> My moisture, and my vital heat,
> In me, do now begin to cease.
> My pulses out of Order beat;
> Strength fails, and Weakness doth increase.

While the physical body can only look forward to 'In darkness, and in stench thou lie, /Where worms thy feature shall deface, /And make thee loathsome to the eye,' the Christian is ultimately comforted with thoughts of eternity:

> Know'st thou, what follows after Death,
> Thou could'st not love this airy Breath.
> Thou shalt in beauty pass the Stars;
> And no defect on thee shall rest,
> Thou shalt be swifter than the Spheres;
> And wear perfections of the best.[85]

The other two sections of *Haleluiah* culminate a vision of a life absorbed into vocal music. Wither's early Anglicanism supports the liturgical calendar in 'Hymns Temporal': this section includes songs for such traditional feasts as Rogation Day, Trinity Sunday, and saints' days, as well as days of the week, birthdays, and anniversaries. Introducing the more idiosyncratic 'Hymns Personal,' the author acknowledges that these songs might have a doubtful reception: 'they will not seem so plausible as Occasional and Temporary Hymns; which have been very anciently in use.' He hopes they will not be considered frivolous 'novelties,' but used rather 'to insinuate into persons of every Calling and Degree, some of those Musings and Considerations, which are necessary to be remembered. This

---

[84] George Wither, *Haleluiah, or Britan's Second Remembrancer, bringing to Remembrance (in praisefull and Penitentiall Hymns, Spirituall Songs, and Morall-Odes) Meditations, advancing the glory of God in the practise of Pietie and Vertue; and applyed to easie Tunes, to be Sung in Families, &c.* (London, 1641), 108.

85 Ibid., 109.

way as I thought instruction might be received with most ease, and least offence.'[86] Wither then proceeds to re-create the imagined experiences and emotions of a variety of stations, including 'For a Magistrate,' 'For a Courtier,' 'For a Servant,' 'For Orphans,' 'For a Husband,' 'For a Wife,' 'For a Lawyer,' 'For a Musician,' 'For a Nurse,' 'For a Labourer,' 'For a Cripple,' and (the most adventurous) 'For them who intend to settle in Virginia, New England, or the like places.' 'For Lovers being constrained to be absent from each other,' reveals a glimpse into mores of courtship in seventeenth-century England: Wither warns 'Lovers tempted by carnal desires' to 'climb to affections, more sublime.' 'For one contentedly married,' sings the joys of married companionship, and another hymn offers comfort 'For a Widower, or a Widow deprived of a loving Yoke-fellow.'

While bereavement is a universal sentiment, and present in Western literature long before *Haleluiah*—Christine de Pisan's fourteenth-century verse on the death of her husband is one example—the next title offers something different. Here we have the more complex subject of someone whose marriage was *not* so happy: 'For a Widower, or a Widow delivered from a troublesome Yoke-fellow.' We can imagine what such a person would be feeling—relief from being finally relieved of a stifling, binding relationship? Perhaps guilt over having not loved the partner enough? Wither's song reflects this ambiguity. He writes in preface: 'Because deliverance from a troublesome Yoke-fellow, is a benefit neither to be despised nor undiscreetly rejoiced in; this Hymn teacheth with what moderation, with what tenderness of heart, and with what desire we should be affected in such cases.' As befits bereavement, it should be sung 'as the Lamentation.' The words acknowledge the relief someone would feel:

> Rejoice not without fear, my heart,
> That, thou by death's impartial stroke,
> Discharged from thy partner art,
> And, freed from an unequal Yoke.

The song ends with a warning for better choices in the future: 'And, if thy providence allows /Another helper unto me; /Lord, keep us faithful in our vows, /Both to each other, and to thee.'[87]

Finally, some of the lyrics in *Haleluiah* depict the most intimate and personal emotions possible. 'For one whose Beauty is much praised,' 'For one upbraided with Deformity,' 'When a Woman hath conceived,' 'For Parents hopeful of Children,' 'For such as are Barren,' 'When a dear Friend is deceased,' and, most touchingly, 'For Parents who have lost their children.' Except for those who have experienced such loss, it is impossible

---

86 Ibid., 345.
87 Ibid., 408.

to imagine the depths of grief and pain a bereaved parent feels. That Wither assumed that people could, and perhaps should, actually *sing*—not only cry—in the midst of such sorrow indicates how gracious and profound he considered the voice's function to be upon the deepest recesses of the personality. During an era of high infant mortality, in the same century when Thomas Hobbes would write that human existence was, on the main, 'solitary, poor, nasty, brutish, and short,' these songs by Wither quietly suggest that individual lives do matter, do make some difference in the cosmos—no matter how humble the station or class.

Three decades after *Haleluiah* was first published, John Bunyan's religious allegory *The Pilgrim's Progress* fired the imaginations of English readers. While Bunyan's work has been described as a classic example of the Puritan anguish of conscience, it was quite popular among Anglicans as well, and charities under the Church of England showed a measure of quasi-official support for the book's evangelical doctrines by distributing it as part of their literacy programs.[88] As with *The Court of Vertue* and *Haleluiah*, the English Reformed tradition of empathetic singing lies at the center of *The Pilgrim's Progress*. Whenever the hero's journey leads him through an especially treacherous episode, the narrative stops while the character pauses to sing a short meditation. Bunyan patterns the same habit of memorializing archetypal, spiritual experience through vocalization—specifically, through song. In the following ditty, Christian rejoices after escaping the Valley of the Shadow of Death:

> O world of wonders! (I can say no less),
> That I should be preserv'd in that distress
> That I have met with here! Oh, blessed be
> That hand that from it hath delivered me!
> Dangers in darkness, Devils, Hell, and Sin
> Did compass me, while I this Vale was in;
> Yea, Snares, and Pits, and Traps, and Nets did lie
> My path about, that worthless silly I
> Might have been catch't intangled, and cast down:
> But since I live, let JESUS wear the Crown.[89]

Simple and sentimental, Bunyan's verses feature a preponderance of the first person singular, thereby encapsulating the cosmic drama of salvation and bringing it down to a personal level. Although *The Pilgrim's Progress* contains no musical notation, it conveys a lively impression of a faith which

---

88 Jeremy Gregory, 'Anglicanism and the arts: religion, culture and politics in the eighteenth century,' in *Culture, Politics and Society in Britain, 1660-1800*, Jeremy Black and Jeremy Gregory, eds. (Manchester: Manchester University Press, 1991), 90.

89 John Bunyan, *The Pilgrim's Progress* (London, 1678), 84.

finds natural expression through music. It has been suggested that Bunyan's underlying motive for inserting these songs into his allegory was really an apologetic one—that he was writing in defense of hymn-singing during a time when many English Baptist congregations (among them, his own chapel in Bedford) were mired in controversy over the subject.[90] Bunyan was also reflecting common practice, for by the latter seventeenth century singing had become indispensable to the English Protestant experience. His allegory confirms that this vocal aesthetic continued to exert a powerful influence over the culture, even after the nation had been torn apart by religious wars and purges.

This same tradition of personalized song lyrics later birthed the hymns of Isaac Watts, Charles Wesley, and the English Victorians, which together have made an incalculable impact upon the spiritual lives of many. As Bunyan commented in *Light for them that sit in Darkness*, 'Peace ... is expressed by singing, because the peace of God when it is received into the soul by faith putteth the conscience into a heavenly and melodious frame.'[91] How the voice was specifically believed to do this—its simultaneous ability to both manifest and affect the inner life—is the subject of the next chapter.

---

90 U. Milo Kaufmann, *The Pilgrim's Progress and Traditions in Puritan Meditation* (New Haven: Yale University Press, 1966), 222. Kaufmann's book concludes with a chapter on aural features of Bunyan's work, where he writes: 'The fact is that the aural orientation toward the Word, with the Scripture a voice for the inner ear, proved remarkably congenial to a conception of meditation as inner oratory, in which the voice was not necessarily that of Scripture but might be that of the spiritual or rational self expostulating with the sensuous nature,' 240. And: 'Puritanism's orientation toward the aural is an integral part of the total picture we have been elaborating, and basic to the composition is the conviction that God speaks. Revelation in word rather than spectacle or event enjoyed the determinacy and rationality as well as the intimacy of personal address so desired by the Puritan ... the Bible was first of all a speaking word addressed to each reader; meditation that amplified upon the text or moved to other subjects ordinarily preserved the nexus of voice and ear, with devotee both speaker and audience,' 249.

91 John Bunyan, *Light for them that sit in Darkness* (1675); quoted in Christopher Hill, *A Tinker and a Poor Man* (New York: Alfred A. Knopf, 1989), 260.

Chapter Three

Sounding the Inner Landscape

'Singing disposes the Affections to follow Reason, more readily and more vigorously than they would if they had not the assistance of a favourable Imagination.'
—Henry Dodwell, *A Treatise concerning the Lawfulness of Instrumental Musick in Holy Offices*

'A Man knows no more in Religion, than he loves and embraceth with the affections of his soul.'
— Richard Sibbes, *Light from Heaven*

As the separation of fields of learning into neat and distinct disciplines was a tendency foreign to early modern scholarship, an Anglican or Puritan devotional work from this era might typically offer, alongside its practical theology, excursions of the author upon a variety of topics, ranging from ancient history, contemporary social customs, the proper place and function of the arts, politics, the natural sciences, family relationships, to what is now known as psychology. This last subject now comes to the fore as we examine early English Protestant theories about the anatomy of the soul, and the profound influence that vocal expression, especially singing, was believed to hold over it. The devotion of this culture features many vocal signifiers, some obvious, others less so; and it is my contention that all of these, taken together, reveal an intimate relationship between period concepts of the voice and concepts of the inner life.

Background: Music and the Motions of the Soul

The idea that music, in its generic sense, has the capacity to express and stir the deepest human passions was a commonplace during the time in which these English devotional writers lived, and it was a sentiment which they themselves embraced and articulated frequently. Secular English musical philosophy from the late sixteenth century to the early eighteenth century featured a complex synthesis of the ancient theories of Pythagoras, Plato, Aristotle, and Boethius, as well as contributions from medieval and Renaissance-era figures, including Zarlino, Vicentino, and other Italian humanists who formed the Florentine Camerata and ultimately fostered the genre of opera. Two historic strains of thought, in particular, dealt with the question of music's influence over emotional states. The first, derived variously from the theories of Plato and Aristotle, concerned music's mimetic power upon the human personality, for good and ill. As Aristotle commented centuries earlier, 'Rhythm and melody supply imitation of ... qualities of character, which hardly fall short of the actual affections, as we know from our own experience, for in listening to such strains our souls undergo a change.'[1] The second line of influence, stemming from Pythagorean numerical proportions and developed further by Boethius, was the idea that the soul has a natural sympathy with music by virtue of the soul's mystical connection to *musica mundana*, the harmony of the spheres—a universal harmony of which perceptible music was believed to be but one facet. A persistently long-lasting force in intellectual history, Pythagorean musical theory withstood both the refutations of Johannes de Grocheo in the fourteenth century, and the more recent inroads of Copernican and Newtonian astronomy, to retain a respectable presence in early modern England. John Dowland refers to it in his *Second Book of Airs* when he calls music 'the Noblest of all Sciences: for the Whole frame of Nature is nothing but Harmony, as well in Souls as bodies.'[2] Even at the end of the seventeenth century, when Enlightenment thinking was stretching across Europe, John Dryden still drew upon Pythagorean imagery for his poems 'A Song for St. Cecilia's Day, 1687,' and 'An Ode, on the Death of Mr. Henry Purcell' (1695).

> From harmony, from heav'nly harmony
> This universal frame began:
> From harmony to harmony
> Thro' all the compass of the notes it ran,
> The diapason closing full in Man.
> —A Song for St. Cecilia's Day, 1687

For official Anglican opinion on the subject of abstract music's power upon the affections no better source exists than Richard Hooker's *Laws of Ecclesiastical Polity*. The Elizabethan theologian acknowledges

> An admirable facility which music hath to express and represent to the mind, more inwardly than any other sensible mean, the very standing, rising, and falling, the very steps and inflections every way, the turns and varieties of all passions whereunto the mind is subject ... In harmony the very image and character even of virtue and vice is perceived, the mind delighted with their resemblances, and brought by having them often iterated into a love the things themselves. For which cause there is nothing more contagious and pestilent than some kinds of harmony; than some nothing more strong and potent unto good ... there is that draweth

---

1 Aristotle, *Politics* 1340, a-b, Jowett, tr.; quoted in Gretchen Finney, 'Ecstasy and Music in Seventeenth-Century England,' *Journal of the History of Ideas* 8 (April 1947), 159.

2 John Dowland, preface to *Second Book of Airs*.

to a marvellous grave and sober mediocrity, there is also that carrieth as it were into ecstasies, filling the mind with a heavenly joy and for the time in a manner severing it from the body.[3]

Francis Rous gives another example of Christian/Pythagorean musical imagery (in this case expressed through his Puritan affectionate style) where he describes the ideal condition of a believer's soul:

The highest and happiest, and sweetest harmony is, when the soul is in a unison with her Saviour and husband: every touch and sound of the soul thus tuned to Christ Jesus, resoundeth in him, toucheth and moveth him. And as with the sound of outward music the spirit of God came upon the Prophet; so with the sound of this inward music (be it in holy contemplations, ardencies, desires, in vocations, resolutions) the Spirit of Christ Jesus cometh more powerfully and plentifully into the soul.[4]

The Case of Vocal Music

While early modern English thought concerning music's power over the affections thus lay well within the received Western philosophical tradition, the devotional culture of the time contributed an aggressive re-focus upon singing, the most ancient form of musical expression. It is no coincidence that vocal music always received the bulk of English Protestant theological attention. An enduring controversy over whether singing was, indeed, the *only* permittable form of church music fascinated many onlookers and fostered a great deal of lively debate throughout the age. Many Puritans and Nonconformists (although bishop Jeremy Taylor, author of the Anglican classics *Holy Living* and *Holy Dying*, was also among this number) voiced suspicion over the use of musical instruments in public worship, and questioned whether music without text was allowable in church under New Testament ordinances. Those who held this opinion, not wishing to confuse the fruits of human invention with God's power, tended to downplay or distrust music's ability to raise the soul to rapture and ecstasy;[5] they rather preferred vocal music because it was inseparably connected to an inspired text and thus, in their view, had a far greater efficacy—a supernatural one.[6]

---

3 Hooker, *Ecclesiastical Polity*, bk. 5, 38:1.
4 Rous, *The Mysticall Marriage*, 288.
5 *Ekstasis*, the state in which the soul 'exceeds itself.'
6 Gretchen Finney has remarked that divines who aligned themselves on this side of the church music controversy, whether they knew it or not, 'had many attitudes in common with the musician and with the poet who were moulding the 'new style' in music, especially in Italy, even with Plato, whose statement that, 'Melody and rhythm will depend upon the words' had inspired the sixteenth-century Italian composer.' ' "Organical Musick" and Ecstasy,' *Journal of the History of Ideas* 8 (June 1947): 291.

On the other side of the question lay the majority of Anglican leaders who, citing the use of timbrels and other exotic instruments in the temple worship of the Old Testament, and furthermore tending to conflate music's capacity to move the affections with the divine work of grace, saw nothing wrong with the presence of instruments in church, and cast an equally mild eye upon the occasional melismatic or *bravura* passage in service music.

Thus the battle lines of an aesthetic argument were drawn. After the Restoration, Anglicans increasingly distanced themselves from their dissenting brethren by emphasizing and even exploiting to their own advantage this artistic point of difference (even though Baxter and some other Nonconformists did approve of the use of church organs); it is interesting to note to what extent the party line of a late seventeenth-century ecclesiastical establishment continues to shape the modern perception of Puritanism as a rabidly anti-musical ideology. Yet the fact remains that beyond the world of denominational identity, theological controversies, and partisan St. Cecilia's Day sermons, English Protestants —never mind their opinion on what music should be performed on Sunday mornings—were unified by their fascination with the singing voice. The record testifies that even sticklers on the subject of instruments in church waxed enthusiastic about the possibilities for spiritual transformation implicit in singing. We should not be surprised when we often find, in period discussions of the soul, the subject of singing looming somewhere near the horizon.

Incidentally, the presence of such differences within the culture does not detract from the viability of the musical life it did have. Even if zealots had succeeded in abolishing all instrumental music in England (an extreme no one ever proposed), modern scholars could still find ample material in the seventeenth-century song repertory—vocal music is, after all, no less valid than instrumental music. Furthermore, as these controversies dealt primarily with public worship, they did not dampen private and family musical activities, nor affect the new venues of music meetings and concerts.

The power accorded to vocal music in early English Protestant culture owed a great deal to its inherent relationship with words, invisible substances which, as we saw in chapter two, were believed to hold great power in themselves. Theological and secular writings of the period agree that during singing the capacity of music to raise the affections combines with the force of words to create a potent agent for moral and spiritual change. Since the apostle Paul 'particularly enjoins Singing the Psalms, Hymns, and Spiritual Songs, as tending to promote the Interest of Holiness in our Hearts and Lives,' divines knew that the idea had clear scriptural warrant.[7] During the late sixteenth century, a heady era when English reformers were asking fundamental questions about the place of music in

---

7 Jabez, 'Of the Nature of the Duty of Singing,' in *Practical Discourses of Singing*, 2.

life and society, a work entitled *The Praise of Musicke* revived the teachings of Isidor, Justin Martyr, Athanasius, Chrysostom, and especially Augustine: 'all the affections of our Spirits have certain proper motions *in the voice and song*, according to the sweet diversity thereof, which ... are excited and stirred up' [emphasis added].[8] The bishop of Hippo's words would become a prevailing theme throughout the period. A decade later, Thomas Morley in *A Plaine and Easy Introduction to Practical Musicke* describes singing's power over the affections:

> All [music] which are made on a ditty [with words] requireth most art, and moveth and causeth most strange effects in the hearer, being aptly framed for the ditty and well expressed by the singer, for it will draw the auditor (and especially the skillful auditor) into a devout and reverent kind of consideration of him for whose praise it was made.[9]

This line of thought survives a century later in a pedadogical treatise which flatly pairs singing with the affections:

> Vocal Music is an Art of expressing rightly things by Voice, for the sweet moving of the affections and the mind ... Singing ... directeth the understanding ... The end and effect of it is, a sweet moving of the affections and the mind. For exhilarating the animal spirits, it moderateth gratefully the affections, and thus penetrateth the interiours of the mind, which it most pleasantly doth affect.[10]

Still later, at the beginning of the eighteenth century, Arthur Bedford in *The Great Abuse of Music* compliments Henry Playford's *Harmonia Sacra* as being 'the most proper Entertainment for the Devout,' and the 'very Glory and Perfection of Music.' Singing these songs is therapeutic, Bedford asserts, because 'our Affections stand in as great need of Helps to raise our Devotion, and fix our Thoughts on heavenly Things, because of their natural Aversion, so that some Care ought to be taken to influence them aright.'[11]

Singing offers the benefits of solace and comfort. Ravenscroft's assertion that 'the singing of Psalms comforteth the sorrowful' was echoed in countless psalters and controversial writings of the time. Singing becomes a therapeutic balm for the soul and healer of personal problems. Along these lines, divines recommended evening as the best time to sing in one's private 'closet':

> When we are Afflicted very much, be the occasions what they will, what Consolations of God, which are not small, may we find in our Spiritual

---

8 *The Praise of Musicke* (London, 1586), 71.
9 Morley, *A Plaine and Easie Introduction,* 179.
10 A.B. Philo-Mus., *Synopsis of Vocal Musick* (London, 1680), 1.
11 Arthur Bedford, *The Great Abuse of Music* (London, 1711), 221.

Songs, which God our maker has given us for the Night, of those Dark hours, which our Afflictions may bring upon us?[12]

Throughout these and other excerpts, the act of singing is increasingly linked with broader aims of moral cultivation and pruning of the soul. As we delve deeper into this literature, we find more than a restatement of ancient teachings; we discover, rather, a sophisticated network of belief underlying musical practice.

'Me thinks I should see his soul ready to fly out of his mouth in an heavenly ravishment': The Verbal Orientation of Early English Protestantism

It is no coincidence that the English fascination with devotional singing existed simultaneously with a strong verbal and aural orientation within early Protestant theology and practice. This abiding societal interest in vocal expression—speech as well as song—was a result of several different factors: some of them secular and thus shared by English and Continental society at-large, some of them theological and pietistic and hence more unique to the religious culture.

Foremost among the secular forces at work was the tremendous influence of rhetoric upon the arts and the educational system. Aristotle, Cicero, and Quintilian had written extensively on oratory and rhetoric, defining and codifying the discipline, and medieval scholars confirmed its relevance by placing it within the Trivium. During the Renaissance, rhetoric underwent a revival of sorts, due in part to the discovery of Quintilian's long-lost *Institutio oratia* in a cell at St. Gall in 1416. The work was quickly disseminated throughout Italy and across Europe, and became the most influential classical and rhetorical manual in use through the Renaissance and Baroque eras. An emphasis upon rhetorical studies was to dominate European educational curricula until the early nineteenth century.

Much of the challenge of effective communication consists in matching a suitable delivery of words with their actual, true meaning. It is ridiculous, rhetoricians would argue, for a lover to declare his feelings in a stern or disinterested voice: what he wants, after all, is a favorable response from his lady. Persuasion is the ultimate goal of rhetoric, and in order to persuade, one must move the passions of one's hearers—and the vehicle for this persuasion is the physical voice. During this era we see discussions of rhetoric being linked with the voice in a more concrete way. Along these lines, the Roman Catholic writer Thomas Wright cites the particular effectiveness of a well-modulated voice in his 1604 treatise *The Passions of the Minde in Generall*:

---

12 Mather, *Accomplished Singer*, 9.

The passion passeth not only through the eyes, but also pierceth the ear, and thereby the heart; for a flexible and pliable voice, accommodated in manner correspondent to the matter whereof a person intreateth, conveyeth the passion most aptly, pathetically, & almost harmonically, & every accent, exclamation, admiration, increpation, indignation, commiseration, abhomination, examination, exultation, fitly (that is, distinctly, at time and place, with gesture correspondent, and flexibility of voice proportionate) delivered, is either a flash of fire to incense a passion, or a basin of water to quench a passion incensed.[13]

In theoretical writings throughout the early modern period, music (especially vocal music) retains close ties with her sister arts of poetry and oratory. The pairing had ancient antecedents, as Quintilian had linked music and rhetoric together when he wrote that the two arts vary in both tone and rhythm,

Expressing sublime thoughts with elevation, pleasing thoughts with sweetness, and ordinary with gentle utterance, and in every expression of its art is in sympathy with the emotions of which it is the mouthpiece. It is by the raising, lowering or inflection of the voice that the orator stirs the emotions of his hearers, and the measure ... of voice and phrase differs according as we wish to rouse the indignation or the pity of the judge. For, as we know, different emotions are roused even by the various musical instruments, which are incapable of reproducing speech.[14]

Present-day musicologists agree that rhetoric has contributed more to Western musical thought than was previously guessed, and it is now recognized that early music specialists should have some basic knowledge of rhetorical theory. Song scholarship in recent years has tended to concentrate on two aspects in particular: *decoratio* —in musical terms, the use of figures to express textual meanings (once reduced to mere 'madrigalisms' or 'word painting'); and *pronuntiatio*, the performance or delivery of an oration—related to the gestural and performance practice traditions of Renaissance and baroque singing.[15]

---

13 Wright, *Passions of the Mind*, 175.
14 Quintilian, *Institutio Oratoria* (1.10.22-7), tr. H.E. Butler, 4 vols. (London, 1920-2; 1963); quoted in Vickers, 372.
15 According to rhetoric, the four steps to successful argument are: 1) *inventio,* 2) *dispositio,* 3) *decoratio,* and 4) *pronuntiatio.* In musical terms, *inventio* and *dispositio* have been traditionally applied to composition, as a composer invents a melodic idea, or subject, and then develops and arranges it. The next step, *elocutio* or *decoratio* is seen to relate to the use of musical-rhetorical devices within a piece. *Memoria* (to memorize) is self-explanatory. For more on rhetoric's influence upon English Renaissance song performance, see Toft, *Tune Thy Musicke*.

The rhetorical paradigm complements one belief in particular: an awe of words as unique vessels of emotion. Concerning the process of musical creation, William Byrd stated that the power within words assisted him in the composition of vocal music:

> There is a certain hidden power, as I learnt by experience, in the thoughts underlying the words themselves, so that as one meditates upon the sacred words and constantly and seriously considers them, the right notes, in some inexplicable manner, suggest themselves quite spontaneously.[16]

This view would easily blend in with any existing theological predisposition towards the voice. The abundant literature on prayer and preaching has much to say on this subject, for both were vocal modes of communication which shared with singing the themes of spiritual integrity, sincerity, and humility—the willingness to act as an obedient vessel. William Fenner thought that preachers owed the words they spoke a correspondingly intense style of delivery: indeed, that the words *demanded* it; and Anglicans and Puritans were in universal agreement that the most important words of all—Holy Scripture—were especially deserving of this kind of thoughtful treatment. Fenner warns that reading the scriptures aloud in a dull manner actually diminishes God's word by robbing it of a crucial aspect of its power:

> The affections of a speech are the soul of a speech, both make up the whole of the Word. 'Is not my Word like unto fire, and like a hammer, that breaketh the rocks in pieces?' ... If the Word be a fire, he that delivers it coldly, delivers the Word otherwise than it is.[17]

While this is reminiscent of directives from rhetorical manuals that speakers must take care to match their oratorical style with the subject, Fenner's implicit assumption that the Word is especially worthy because it is a living and divine force reflects the distinctive Reformed theological tradition chronicled in chapter two. The court preacher John Preston shared Fenner's attitude that holy words are containers of emotional power. Acknowledging in *The Saints Daily Exercise* that God hears and responds to silent prayers, he goes on to cite the special benefits of articulating one's private thoughts out loud: 1) the physical action of speaking stimulates the inner affections 2) it orders potentially unruly thoughts. 'But when there is any cause to use the voice, in private, it is this, as far as it may quicken the heart ... and as far as thereby we may keep our thoughts from wandering.'[18] A similar idea is found in Watts' 'Of the Tone of the Voice in Prayer':

---

16 William Byrd, *Gradualia*, Book I (1605), Fellowes's translation.
17 William Fenner, *A Treatise of the Affections* (London, 1641), 141.
18 John Preston, *The Saints' Daily Exercise: A Treatise Unfolding the Whole Dutie of Prayer* (London, 1629), 86.

I confess, in secret prayer there is no necessity of a voice, for God hears a whisper as well as a sigh and a groan. Yet some Christians cannot pray with any advantage to themselves without the use of a voice in some degree; nor can I judge it at all improper, but rather preferable, so that you have a convenient place for secrecy: for hereby you will not only excite your own affections the more, but by the practice in secret, if you take due care of your voice there, you may learn also to speak in public the better.[19]

The seventeenth-century Puritan John Owen wrote some of the lengthiest and most detailed enquiries into the nature of prayer in early English Protestant devotional literature, and he did not leave the question of the voice untouched. In *A Discourse of the Work of the Holy Spirit in Prayer* he proposes that the act of verbalization in prayer excites the affections and disciplines the imagination through a mutual 'recoiling of efficacy.'

Words proper, suggested by the Spirit of God, and taken either Directly or Analogically out of Scripture, do help the mind and enlarge it with Supplications ... The use of such Words, being first led unto by the desires of the mind, may and doth lead the mind on to express its further desires also, and increaseth those which are so expressed. It is from God's Institution and blessing that the Minds and will of praying do lead unto the Words of Prayer, and the words of Prayer do lead on the mind and will, enlarging them in desires and supplications. And without this Aid, many would oftentimes be strait'ned in acting their Thoughts and Affections towards God, or distracted in them, or diverted from them. And we have experienced that an obedient, sanctified persistency in the use of gracious words in Prayer, hath prevailed against violent Temptations and injections of Satan, which the mind in its silent contemplations was not able to grapple with: and holy Affections are thus also excited thereby. The very words and expressions which the Mind chooseth to declare its thoughts, conceptions, and desires about Heavenly things, do reflect upon the Affection's increasing and exciting of them. Not only the things themselves fixed on, do affect the heart, but the Words of Wisdom and sobriety whereby they are expressed, do so also. There is a recoiling of Efficacy, if I may so speak, in deep impressions on the affections, from the words that are made use of to express those Affections by.[20]

---

19 Isaac Watts, 'A Guide to Prayer,' in *The Beauties of the late Reverend Dr. Isaac Watts*, 146.

20 John Owen, *A Discourse of the Work of the Holy Spirit in Prayer. With a brief Enquiry into the Nature and Use of Mental Prayer and Forms* (London, 1682), 193.

Within this context, singing was considered more effective than plain speech because in singing words were celebrated with 'more glory.'[21] Hence the act of phonation and the articulation of words were activities heavily weighted with significance by early modern English culture. Another influence contributing to this vocal orientation was the traditional superiority of sound as a conduit of knowledge. Western tradition considered hearing in many respects to be the most privileged of all the senses. Aristotle wrote in *De Sensu*: 'Seeing, regarded as a supply for the wants of life, and its direct effects, is the superior sense; but for developing intelligence, and in indirect consequences, hearing takes the precedence.'[22] The sixteenth-century treatise *Exotericae exercitationes* pronounced, 'We learn things through the hearing more easily than through the sight, because the voice affects us more by inflection and insinuating itself into the sense.'[23] In the seventeenth century Francis Bacon noted that 'the Sense of Hearing striketh the Spirits more immediately, than the other Senses; And more incorporeally than the Smelling.'[24] The seventeenth-century Anglican preacher Humfrey Sydenham remarked upon the useful immediacy of musical sound:

> *Sonus ipse*, the very sound itself ... passeth through the ears, and by them unto the heart ... So that although we lay altogether aside the consideration of Ditty or Matter, the very murmur of sounds rightly modulated and carried through the porches of our ears to those spiritual rooms within, is by a native vigour more than ordinarily powerful, both to move and moderate all affections.[25]

A preference for the sense of hearing existed as well in the era's theology. It is interesting that the condition of being 'called' by God (according to Reformed doctrine, the initial step of conversion) is an auditory image. The same divine Voice, which boomed forth the word by which planets and galaxies were created, was also thought to foster the creation of new life within the believer's soul. Both Old and New Testaments use the word 'hear' in the urgent sense of 'listen very carefully

---

21 Homes, *Gospel Musick*, 12.
22 Aristotle, *De sensu* 1, 437a4-6; quoted in Penelope Gouk, 'Some English Theories of Hearing in the Seventeenth Century: Before and After Descartes,' in *The Second Sense: Studies in Hearing and Musical Judgement from Antiquity to the Seventeenth Century*, Charles Burnett, Michael Fend and Penelope Gouk, eds. (London: The Warburg Institute, University of London, 1991), 100.
23 J.C. Scaliger, *Exotericarum exercitationum liber XV de subtilitate, ad Hieronymum Cardanum* (Paris, 1557), f. 369r (Ex. 298.1); quoted in Gouk, 100.
24 Francis Bacon, *Sylva*, experiments 101-3, 128, 168; quoted in Gouk, 103.
25 Hymphrey Sydenham, *The Well-Tuned Cymball, Or, a Vindication of the Moderne Harmony and Ornaments in our Churches. Against the Murmuring of their discontented Opposers* (London, 1637), 39.

to what is being said,' and the special efficacy of the aural mode is further supported by Romans 10:17: 'Faith cometh by hearing, and hearing by the word of God.' Commenting upon this verse, Richard Alleine contrasts the spiritual woes which come through sight against the benefits which come through the ear:

> How came Sin and death into this world, and all the Plagues and miseries we are labouring under, or liable to? Which way came they in? By the eye they came in: when the Woman [saw] the fatal Apple, then she lusted and tasted …
>
> How came Life and Immortality, Grace and peace, and all our glorious Hopes in again? By the ear, they came in: By this the Promise entered, by this Faith entered.[26]

In like manner, Joseph Hall remarks that through the ear come the specifics of gospel truth: 'Our eye is our best guide to God our Creator, but our ear is it that leads us to God our Redeemer. How shall they believe except they hear?'[27] Daniel Featley chides, 'Hast thou an ear (O Christian by thy profession) for the Devil, and none for God?'[28] According to Hall and others, the outer ear exists parallel with a metaphorical, inner ear of the soul, which becomes truly receptive only when captured and penetrated by the Holy Spirit:

> It is the charge of the Spirit, Let him that hath an ear hear; Every one hath not an ear, and of those that have an ear, every one heareth not; The soul hath an ear as well as the body; if both these ears do not meet together in one act, there is no hearing … The outward ear may be open, and the inward shut; if way be not made through both, we are deaf to spiritual things. Mine ear hast thou boared, or digged, saith the Psalmist; the vulgar reads it, my ears hast thou perfited [perfected]: Surely our ears are grown up with flesh; there is no passage for a perfit [perfect] hearing of the voice of God, till he have made it by a spiritual perforation.[29]

In his commentary on the epistle to the Colossians, Nicholas Byfield points to the special effectiveness of the word heard: 'No man can get eternal graces, or an enduring contentment, arising from the hope of a better life, without the hearing of the word of God.' Next he lists the ten benefits of hearing the word:

1) It causes the Holy Ghost to come upon the listeners
2) It opens up the heart
3) It makes the fear of God descend

---

26 Richard Alleine, *The World Conquered* (London, 1668), 293-94.
27 Joseph Hall, *The Devout Soul, or Rules of heavenly devotion* (London, 1644), 95.
28 Featley, *Ancilla Pietatis*, 59.
29 Joseph Hall, *The Devout Soul*, 103.

4) It tames and melts the 'proud and stony-heart'
5) It begets faith
6) It seals believers by the Holy Spirit of promise
7) It provides the vehicle whereby the Spirit speaks to the churches
8) It allows Christ to 'come sup with men'
9) It cures a grieved conscience
10) It brings life and salvation.[30]

Thus the Puritan exhortation to 'hear the word' whenever possible, plus the habit among some of traveling great distances to attend sermons, both represent practical outgrowths of this theological legacy. Anglicanism had its tradition of great preachers as well in the court chaplains Donne and Andrewes, and the devout Anglican apparently enjoyed hearing a good sermon as well as any Puritan.

The voice also gained attention through numerous works of practical theology on the tongue. Being predominantly concerned with the mechanics of human relationships, or the 'second table' of God's commandments, this genre focuses upon the virtues of pure, sincere speech while excoriating gossip, slander, lying, blasphemy, and other forms of 'false talk.' The tongue figures prominently in scripture commentaries as well. The book of Proverbs alone provides much material on this subject: for example, the tongue of the just is as silver (Prov. 10:20), the tongue of the wise is health (Prov. 12:18), and the wholesome tongue is a tree of life (Prov. 15:4); yet a lying tongue is 'but for a moment' (Prov. 12:29), and the tongue contains the power of death as well as life ((Prov. 18:21). The epistle of James was another favorite text: 'if any man among you seem to be religious, and bridleth not his tongue, but deceiveth his own heart, this man's religion is vain' (James 1:26). It later compares the tongue to a bit in a horse's mouth—a small thing which turns about the entire body—and also to the helm controlling a large ship. In short, the tongue is capable of 'unruly evil, full of deadly poison' (James 3:8).

English divines took their cues from scripture on this subject. Another clergyman who wrote extensively about speech was Thomas Adams.[31] In a sermon entitled 'The Taming of the Tongue,' he remarks that the tongue 'hath the preeminence of all mortal creatures,' and 'it is Little in substance, yet *great ad affectum,* to provoke passion; *ad affectum,* to produce action.'[32] God made it uniquely powerful:

---

30 Nicholas Byfield, *An Exposition Upon the Epistle to the Colossians* (London, 1617), 49.

31 Whom the Romantic poet Robert Southey honored as 'the prose Shakespeare of puritan theologians ... scarcely inferior to Fuller in wit or to Taylor in fancy.'

32 Thomas Adams, *The Sacrifice of Thankefulnesse* (London, 1616), 24, 28.

To create so little a piece of flesh, and to put such vigour into it: to give it neither bones nor nerves, yet to make it stronger than arms and legs, and those most able and serviceable parts of the body ... so on this little weak member hath the Lord conferred the greatest strength: and as feeble as it is, we find it both more necessary, and more honorable.[33]

Adams speculates that something about the act of vocalization itself seems (within human experience) to enlarge the existence and attributes of God—while simultaneously admitting that He cannot be enlarged, being infinitely great already. In this respect, the voice serves an important creative function in its own right:

We that cannot make his name greater, can make it seem greater: and though we cannot enlarge his glory, we can enlarge the manifestation of his glory. This both in words praising, and in works practising. We know it is impossible to make a new Christ ... yet our holy lives, and happy lips (if I may so speak) may make a little Christ, a great Christ. They that before little regarded him, may thus be brought to esteem him greatly: giving him the honour due to his name, and glorifying him, after our example. This is the Tongue's office.[34]

He goes on to comment that of a good tongue, 'there is nothing better,' and of an evil one, 'nothing worse.' Something about its nature prompts only extremes: it is either all good, or all bad. If good, 'it is a walking garden ... an herb of grace to the hearers'; if evil, 'a wild Bedlam, full of gaddings and madding mischiefs.'[35] Adams also believed that God rewards vocalized prayers more than silent prayers: 'It is that instrument which the Holy Ghost useth in us, to cry *Abba Father*. It is our spokesman: and he that can hear the heart without a tongue, regardeth the devotions of the heart better, when they are sent up by a diligent messenger, a faithful tongue.'[36]

A few decades after *The Taming of the Tongue,* Richard Baxter covered similar ground in his popular *Christian Directory.* He cites both classical and biblical writers to explain why the tongue lies superior above all organs: 'Paul saith, "The weapons of our warfare are mighty through God": and Pythagoras could say that "Tongues cut deeper than swords, because they reach even to the soul": Tongue-sins and duties therefore must needs be great.'[37] Baxter continues: 'The tongue is made to be the Index or expresser of the mind,' and concludes that it affects the mind and heart in equal strength:

---

33 Ibid., 29.
34 Ibid., 23.
35 Ibid., 25.
36 Ibid., 26.
37 Baxter, *A Christian Directory,* 408.

The use of all our highest faculties, parts and graces are expressively by the Tongue: Our Wisdom and Knowledge, our Love and Holiness are much lost as to the Honour of God, and the good of others, if not expressed. The tongue is the Lanthorn [lantern] or Casement of the Soul, by which it looketh out, and shineth unto others. Therefore the sin or duty of so noble an instrument are not to be made light of by any that regard the honour of our Maker.

Our words have a great reflection and operation upon our hearts. As they come from them, so they recoil to them ... Therefore for our own good or hurt, our words are not to be made light of.[38]

Baxter devotes chapter nine of *A Christian Directory* to 'Directions for the Government of the Tongue,' where he lists sixteen distinct uses and duties of the tongue. Using it to sing the praises of God heads the list.[39] Nathanial Homes agrees that 'singing is the making in a special manner man's tongue to be his glory,'[40] and we find this doctrine reflected in sacred song from this period, where 'Awake, my glory' was a common lyric.

The Anatomy of the Soul

All of this leaves the impression that this devotional culture absorbed a variety of influences regarding vocal expression. The subject received a noteworthy amount of attention in sermons and in print; and equally remarkable is the frequency with which the voice kept inserting itself into period discussions of the psychological and spiritual life. The early modern period inherited a venerable tradition of the anatomy of the soul, that hidden topography of invisible forces which was believed to affect and control human behavior. Along with the rest of educated Europe during this time, Anglican and Puritan divines accepted faculty psychology as a matter of course, and used it as a basis for their speculative inquiries into the

---

38 Ibid.

39 According to Baxter, they are: 1) To glorify God, 2) To sing psalms of praise and 'delight our souls in the sweet commemoration of his excellencies,' 3) To give thanks for God's mercies and tell others of them, 4) To pray for the requests of ourselves, our brethren, and the Church, and for the conversion of enemies, 5) To appeal to God and swear by his Name when called to it lawfully, 6) To make holy vows and professions of faith, 7) To preach the word, teach, edify, and correct others, 8) To defend God's truth against error, 9) To exhort, reprove, and encourage others, 10) To confess our sins to God and each other, 11) To seek the advice of others, and to enquire after the will of God, 12) To praise the good in others, and to speak good of all people, 13) To bear witness to the truth, 14) To defend the cause of the just and innocent, vindicate them against false accusers, and excuse deserving causes and people, 15) To communicate the good impressions and affections of mind God has worked within our souls, not the mere intellectual facts, 16) To be the instrument of everyday communication. Ibid, 409.

40 Homes, *Gospel Musick*, 9.

personality. This theory, namely, that the mind is a collection of departments, each with its own separate function, had origins in Aristotle, gained accretions from various ancient and medieval philosophers, and owed a special debt to the categorizing tendencies of medieval scholastics like Albertus Magnus, Duns Scotus, and Aquinas.

Faculty psychology remained the dominant paradigm in sixteenth and seventeenth-century England, although it was eventually challenged by Descartes (who proposed that the mind is a unity with one function) and John Locke's empiricist *An Essay upon the Human Understanding.* Shakespeare's many allusions to this scheme witness to the Elizabethan fascination in general with the bodily humors and diseases of the soul. In music, the preoccupation with the theme of melancholy which permeates the English lute-song literature in the late sixteenth and early seventeenth centuries has led scholars to believe that John Dowland himself—famous for inscribing '*Semper Dowland semper dolens*'—personally suffered from clinical depression. The popularity of Timothy Bright's *Treatise of Melancholy* (1586) and Robert Burton's *The Anatomy of Melancholy* (1621) also shows the dominance of this pre-empirical psychology in the days in which these devotional writers lived and worked.

According to faculty psychology, the soul is a trinity, composed of (in ascending value of worth and uniqueness) a vegetative soul, a sensible soul, and a rational soul. Plants share with humans the characteristics of the vegetative soul, as beasts share qualities of the sensible soul; yet only men and women are endowed with the higher rational capacities of self-consciousness and the gift of language. For example, while a dog quickly learns to expect that each night at dinnertime his bowl will be filled with soft and delicious food, only a human master has the ability to reflect upon this event, write it down, or turn it into a scene of a play. An object initially presents itself to the eye, ear, or some other sense; an image or 'phantasm' of the thing is next carried via the animal spirits to the common sense; from thence it is relayed to the imagination, or fancy (which determines the person's inclination towards or away from the object); it is then stored in the memory (the common sense, imagination, and memory together constitute the 'interior knowing powers'); reason ascertains the image's truth and rightness and sends that judgment to the will (believed to reside 'in the heart') and then commands the affections or passions to work upon the body, finally eliciting some physical response and/or course of action.[41]

When referring to faculty psychology, early modern divines usually passed over its more complicated aspects (such as Aquinas's classification of the concupiscible and irascible appetites) in favor of their own

---

41 I base this paraphrase of faculty psychology on Perry Miller's description in *The New England Mind, The Seventeenth Century* (Cambridge: Harvard University Press, 1954), 240.

innovations (such as William Fenner's version of the nine degrees of human affection).[42] Nonetheless, Anglican and Puritans agreed upon the scheme's basic soundness and often used its terminology. Richard Sibbes gives a classic textbook version in *The Soules Conflict with it Selfe*.[43] Other devotional writers refer to it as well. Baxter in *The Saints' Everlasting Rest* notes that the powers of the soul divide along rational and sensitive categories; Ussher (*A Method for Meditation*), Rous (*The Arte of Happiness*), and Fenner (*A Treatise of the Affections*) all describe the complementary roles of the understanding and the will according to this tradition; and Edward Reynoldes follows faculty psychology to the letter in *A Treatise of the Passions and Faculties of the Soul of Man*.

Anglican and Puritan Methods of Meditation

We might ask at this point whether the adjective *devotional* carries any special significance, or if it is merely synonymous with 'sacred' or 'religious.' Early modern sources use it to refer to an extraordinary degree of spiritual sensitivity, that quality of a soul which actively seeks and follows godliness. The term is integral to the era's conception of the contemplative life. The Anglican Daniel Featley calls devotion

> The heart's warmth, or rather the life's blood of Religion. It is a sacred bond knitting the soul unto God. It is a spiritual muscle moving only upward, and lifting the heart, eyes, and hands continually unto Heaven. And because it consisteth rather in the fervour of the affections … it is better felt than understood, and yet better understood than can be expressed.[44]

Joseph Hall agrees with 'devotion is the life of religion, the very soul of Piety, the highest employment of grace; and no other than the prepossession of heaven by the Saints of God here upon earth.' He distinguishes devotion from mere *religiosity* (a form of works-righteousness according to Hall) which can be measured by such outward factors as frequency, length, or even vehemence. True devotion, rather, is 'an habitual disposition of a holy soul, sweetly conversing with God, in all the forms of an heavenly (yet awful) familiarity; and a constant entertainment of our selves here below

---

42 In Fenner's *A Treatise of the Affections*.

43 'Things work upon the soul in this order: 1. Some object is presented. 2. Then it is apprehended by imagination as good and pleasing, or as evil and hurtful. 3. If good, the desire is carried to it with delight: if evil, it is rejected with distaste, and so our affections are stirred up suitably to our apprehension of the object. 4. Affections stir up the spirits. 5. The spirits raise the humours, and so the whole man becomes moved and oftentimes distempered; this falleth out by reason of the sympathy between the soul and body, whereby what offendeth one redoundeth to the hurt of the other.' Sibbes, *The Soules Conflict with it Selfe*, 162.

44 Featley, *Ancilla Pietatis*, 2.

with the God of spirits, in our sanctified thoughts, and affections.'[45] The state of devotion is viewed primarily as a *condition of being*, not an aggregate of actions. This literature portrays this inner relationship with God as transforming, pleasurable, and accessible to the common believer. In contrast to medieval asceticism, which inferred that the highest form of spirituality was only attainable by a religious elite, possibly cloistered and certainly celibate, Reformed doctrine offered the potential of a life of committed devotion pursued alongside the mundane affairs of marriage, work, and children. To be holy, to be sanctified, to be tenderly 'affectionate'—these ethereal aims were offered freely to all, and the way to achieve them was through regeneration and careful nurture of the inner life. English Protestant meditation thus differs from the esoteric, step-wise path of self-abnegation chronicled by such visionaries as St. John of the Cross and Teresa of Avila; a tradition which hinted that spiritual ecstasy was elusive, fleeting, and possible only after experiencing the mysterious dark night of the soul. Meditation was considered a crucial part of *every* Christian's daily routine. 'Whoever thou art ... that readest these lines,' pleads Baxter,

> I entreat thee in the name of the Lord, as thou valuest the life of constant joy, and that good conscience which is a continual feast, that thou wouldst but seriously set upon this work, and learn the art of heavenly-mindedness, and thou shalt find the increase a hundredfold, and the benefit abundantly exceed thy labour.[46]

Hall charges: 'Brethren, all ye that love God, and his Church, and his Truth, and his Anointed, and your Country, and your selves, and yours, join your forces with mine, and let us by an holy violence make way to the gates of heaven ...'[47] And Sibbes considered meditation vital for the smooth functioning of society, even going so far as to blame its lack for 'many fearful events, strange massacres, and tragical deaths' in England (published in 1638, it is interesting that he wrote this before the civil war).[48] Protestant divines were intrigued by faculty psychology because they had an even greater interest in the cultivation of the inner landscape. What, they wanted to know, actually happens to the soul when it ponders the nature of God and enters into communication with him? How does contemplation relate to, and affect, the outer person? To what extent does the private thought life control self-expression and communication? All of these

---

45 Joseph Hall, *The Devout Soul*, 1.

46 Richard Baxter, *The Saints' Everlasting Rest, or, A treatise of the blessed state of the saints in their enjoyment of God in glory* (London: William Tegg and Co., 1854), 491.

47 Joseph Hall, *The Devout Soul*, preface.

48 Richard Sibbes, *Divine Meditations and Holy Contemplations* (London, 1638), preface.

broader issues were subsumed within the realm of meditation, a dynamic and invisible landscape to this culture, full of intense conflicts and joys, where the soul does battle with the forces of the world, the flesh, and the devil to stay on the right path—a path which finally, happily, leads to paradise.

As so many Anglicans and Puritan thinkers published their own versions of meditation, it is beyond the scope of this book to study each one in detail. We can summarize, however, that they share some important similarities which point to a distinctive English Protestant school of meditation. Prominent ways in which the spirituality transmitted by this literature differed from the Roman Catholic variety include:

1) The ever-present assumption that the common believer should attain a highly sophisticated knowledge of doctrine, which should be practically evinced through signs of sanctification in daily life (even as divines liked to describe this education as 'simple' or 'plain'). Through listening to sermons, engaging in 'holy conversation' with mature believers, and, above all, reading the scriptures and popular devotional books and tracts, a humble laborer or serving maid alike could become a theologically-savvy Christian. The fact that popular literature from the era, such as Ben Jonson's *Bartholmew Fair*, so often held up the bickering and over-scrupulous Puritan as an object of satire proves how deeply this ideal had been embraced by the religious culture.

2) An emphasis upon the invisible aspects of faith, such as 'the true church,' 'the sincere heart,' 'the motions of the soul'; and a corresponding de-emphasis (and, among some Protestants, outright suspicion) of the tangible ecclesiastical establishment and the physical accoutrements of its power like croziers and mitres. This preference paradoxically may account for the early English Protestant fascination with the sensual realm of the body and the natural world, for these were considered *acceptable* (i.e., created by God, not man) corollaries to, and expressions of, the inner life. Moreover, singing was believed to play a significant role in this dichotomy: as one Presbyterian clergyman remarked,

> Singing the Praises of God is very suitable to the Purity of Gospel-Worship, and a very great Exercise of Spirituality. 'Tis a spiritual Object we are wholly to attend, the Glory and Perfection of the Divine Being. We eye him and terminate on him in the most direct and immediate manner ... there is a Concurrence of Soul and Body.[49]

While Puritans and Anglicans disagreed about the validity of 'temple-worship,' even the theological writings of (non-Laudian) Anglican divines during this period display a heightened emphasis on invisible realities over

---

49 Harris, 'The Excellence of the Duty of Singing' in *Practical Discourses of Singing*, 69.

against the material world of ritual *whenever they discuss the fundamentals of faith.* When we think of the Episcopal church today we are viewing it through a post-Tractarian lens, and hence liable to forget how plain much of early Anglican worship actually was.

3) A dislike of too much imposed regimentation upon the inner devotional life. For example, a chapter on cures for melancholy might conclude with the advice that it be taken to heart only if relevant to the reader's own particular condition. In *The Saints' Everlasting Rest*, Baxter leaves many specifics of meditation up to his readers—what topics they choose to concentrate on, the metaphors used, the order of repentance and praise, etc. This individualistic approach distinguishes most early English Protestant writers from the Roman Catholic preference for more detailed schemes in the form of 'ladders,' 'steps,' 'rules,' etc.

4) A seeming distrust of asceticism for its own sake. Though Protestant writers reject 'the flesh' inasmuch as it represents sin, they exhibit little enthusiasm for mortifying the body with lengthy fasts or rigid programs of self-denial. With their stress upon justification by faith, perhaps they feared that too much of an emphasis upon asceticism could become a basis for spiritual pride, or a source of theological confusion—and this could also be a reaction to the previously dominant system of penance and obligations. In relation to this, chapter four will examine how Baxter's treatment of the senses in *The Saints' Everlasting Rest* differs from Augustine's harsher approach in his *Confessions.*

In essence, Anglican and Puritan divines held that the discipline of constant reflection upon the marvelous works of God and his divine decrees leads the believer to an intimate and ever-deepening relationship with the Eternal. While this has been a credo of Christian meditation throughout history, strong sociological and theological tendencies within early English Protestantism grew a distinct branch of contemplative practice. The brief sampler which follows conveys a tone and temperament unique to the Reformation.

One major contributor to the field was the Anglican bishop Joseph Hall, whose devotional titles include *The Art of Divine Meditation, The Devout Soul, An Holy Rapture,* and *Christ Mysticall.* Hall wrote *The Art of Divine Meditation* (1606) at the age of thirty-two after returning from a trip to the continental Lowlands; with this work and others he hoped to establish a new method of contemplation, more acceptable and accessible to English Protestants. In a manual entitled *Select Thoughts* he utilizes a metaphor common to the period when he defines meditation as the anatomy of the digestion of spiritual food, the word of God.

> It is easy to observe that there are five degrees of the digestion of our spiritual food: first it is received into the cell of the ear, and there digested by a careful attention; then it is conveyed into the brain, and there

concocted by due meditation, from thence it is sent down into the heart, and there digested by the affections; and from thence it is conveyed to the tongue, in conference, and holy confession; and lastly, it is thence transmitted to the hand, and there receives perfect digestion, in our action and performance.[50]

Just as the physical body needs to digest food properly for good health, the soul needs to absorb vital spiritual nutrients by following these five steps. Hall goes on to observe that many are spiritually malnourished because their meditations fall short of completion. He names the different levels of spiritual-mindedness: people who completely refuse to listen to the scriptures, who won't 'give as much as ear-room to the word of truth,' he calls *willing recusants;* others who stop at the mere hearing of it, *fashionable auditors;* those who let truth enter their thoughts and memories to an extent, yet fail to act upon that truth, *speculative professors;* those (fewer in number) who entertain a secret liking for holy things in their hearts, but 'hide it in their bosoms, not daring to make profession of it to the world' are *close Nicodemians;* and finally, people who 'take it into their mouths, and busy their tongues in holy chat, yet do nothing,' he dismisses as *formal discoursers.*[51] In this way spiritual nourishment traverses the ear, the brain, the heart, and then the tongue, and is finally 'absorbed' only when the hand is inspired to some appropriate course of action. That Hall inserts this extra step of the tongue into his version of faculty psychology is a significant characteristic evident in other Protestant devotional works as well.

In *The Spirituall Taste Described*, the Puritan Robert Dingley names observation and memory the two main components of meditation. For him, the crux of Christian meditation is contained in these four steps:

> 1) Committing to memory the ways of Providence, 'the hand of God.'
>
> 2) Actively and self-consciously maintaining a storehouse of spiritual memories (related to the common period practice of keeping spiritual diaries).
>
> 3) Constantly recalling these truths to mind, in this way confirming ones' beliefs and discovering new aspects.
>
> 4) Finally, applying the new attitudes and wisdom thus gained to one's own life.[52]

In this way the believer transcends the condition of merely 'seeing' knowledge in order to reach the crucial, experiential 'tasting' of knowledge.

50 Joseph Hall, *Select Thoughts, One Century, also the Breathings of the Devout Soul* (London, 1648), 141.

51 Ibid.

52 Robert Dingley, *The Spirituall Taste Described* (London, 1649), 23.

James Ussher also cites the importance of self-reflection in *A Method for Meditation,* where he describes the sanctified dynamic between the understanding, memory, will, and affections. The memory influences the understanding in much the same way as the affections influence the will. Over all these operations, the *logos* of scripture reigns supreme. This is how Ussher describes the faculties' interplay during meditation:

> There must be first a thinking, a calling to mind, something to feed the understanding, such a morning think on such a point. This course God will wonderfully bless, he will put new thoughts into thee, make such a sin that thou dost meditate of, more hideous and loathsome, than all the reasons in the world could do.
>
> The second work is on the affections, a laying to heart … The first work is calling to mind, debating of the matter. Consider in general such a sin, and the odiousness of it, then lay it to heart, and consider how far thou art guilty of it. Thus apply it close, and home. Now these two things that it may work kindly,
>
> First look backwards, and say, what have I done? Secondly look forwards, and say, what will I do?
>
> First look backwards, what have I done? This is the ground of all the iniquity of the children of Israel … This not looking backwards, makes the Devil to push forwards. And here do not give over till thy heart be broken in the sense of thy sins, God loves this holy boldness. Say as Jacob, I will not part til thou hast blessed me; I will not give over till thou hast broken my heart, given me some repentance, when thus thou hast wrought thy heart pliable, and made it to smite thee; then pour out thy heart in these inexpressible sighs and groans, Rom. 8:26. Whole volleys of sighs, this is a great Ordinance bears down all before it …
>
> Secondly, this being done, look forwards, and say, what will I do? By the grace of God having seen the foulness of sin, the danger of it, shall I continue any longer in it? God forbid. This is a stirring up of the affections.[53]

The Role of Reason

Hall, Dingley, Ussher and other English Protestants stand in basic agreement concerning meditation's techniques and goals. Modern readers might be struck by the prosaic way in which they viewed the subject—we are used to viewing mysticism and reason as separate dichotomies; we prefer to think that metaphysical ecstasies only grace the unwary, that they are fickle in their choice of friends. Yet Sibbes insists that

> Meditation is not a passion of melancholy, nor a fit of fiery love, not covetous care, nor senseless dumps, but a serious act of the Spirit in the

---

53 Ussher, *Method for Meditation,* 38.

inwards of the Soul, whose object is spiritual: whose affection is a
provoked appetite to practise holy things: a kindling in us of the love of
God, a zeal towards his truth, a healing our benumbed hearts.[54]

The term 'a serious act' is revealing, for undergirding this methodical
orientation was always an abiding respect for reason, the throne of the soul,
the king of faculties. Although the Reformers taught that faith is a
supernatural gift from above, the subsequent playing out of that faith was
believed to be closely dependent upon a sanctified but very human
rationality. In other words, while the Fall plunged reason into confusion,
the experience of new life in Christ restores it to its proper intended
function. Baxter explains:

> Though the blindness and disease of reason is contrary to faith and
> holiness, yet Reason it self is so much for it, as that Faith it self is but the
> act of elevated well-informed Reason: and supernatural revelation is but
> the means to inform our Reason, about things which have not a natural
> evidence, discernable by us. And sanctification (actively taken) is but the
> healing of our reason and rational appetite: and Holiness is but the health
> or soundness of them ... to set Reason as Reason in opposition to Faith or
> Holiness, or divine Revelation, is as gross a piece of foolery, as to set the
> visive faculty in opposition to the light of the sun, or to its objects.[55]

Edward Reynoldes concurs with 'Reason is an excellent Instrument to
use those principles of faith unto our further proficiency in sacred
Knowledge, which, without Divine Revelation proposing the Object, and
Divine Grace disposing the Faculty, it could never have either known or
used.'[56] Sibbes calls reason a 'beam of God,' likening its command over the
wayward affections to the calm voice of authority quieting an insurgent
mutiny aboard ship.[57] So the early English Protestant conception of
meditation is not one where the mind is held in complete abeyance while
the more irrational faculties take precedence; rather, the intellect remains
fully engaged.

This has important implications, for throughout the literature we find a
direct connection made between the processes of reason and the voice.
Singing is frequently cited for its skill in disciplining the mind and ordering
the inward thoughts, as 'the sweetness of the lips increaseth learning' (Prov.
16:21). *The Praise of Musicke* states, 'Men do more willingly hear, and
more firmly carry away with them, those things which they hear sung than

---

54 Sibbes, *Divine Meditations,* preface.
55 Richard Baxter, *The Divine Life* (London, 1664), 245.
56 Edward Reynoldes, *A Treatise of the Passions and Faculties of the Soul of Man*
    (London, 1647), 9.
57 Sibbes, *Soules Conflict*, 48.

those which they hear barely spoken and pronounced.'[58] A classic argument was that singing differs from speech inasmuch as it represents a prolongation of speech, and therefore has 'a more distinct and fixed meditation.'[59] William Harris called singing a more effective mode of persuasion because 'the Thoughts have more leisure to work, and are more intensely fixed, while the Sound is dilated and drawn out so great a length, and the Mind employ'd with so much Solemnity.'[60] Pondering how this characteristic of singing relates to meditation, another observed: 'While we are singing, we have a special Opportunity and Help to admonish and instruct our own Souls; as that by dilating the Sound, and prolonging the Voice, there is more time given for the fixing our Hearts upon that which is sung with more delightful Meditation.'[61] John Newman challenged,

> See then, that while your Tongues are employed in charting forth the Words, your Mind and Thoughts be as busily employed in diving into, and in sweet Meditation upon the spiritual Sense and Meaning of them. Unless you have slothful and unengaged Minds, you will find the Duty of Singing a greater help this way, than barely the reading of the words would be, there being a longer time for the exercise of Thought in the one than in the other.[62]

The educational potential of music was not lost upon those responsible for England's spiritual and moral education. It is alluded to in *The Private Devotions of Lancelot Andrewes*, which lists 'the melody of the Psalmer' as one of seven ways in which God instructs the church.[63] Isaac Watts also refers to singing's value as a pedagogical tool in his children's book, *Divine Songs*:

> What is learnt in Verse is longer retain'd in memory, and sooner recollected. The like sounds and the like number of Syllables exceedingly assist the remembrance. And it may often happen, that the end of a Song running in the Mind may be an effectual means to keep off some Temptation: or to incline to some Duty, when a Word of Scripture is not upon the thoughts ... This will be a constant Furniture for the minds of children, that they may have something to think upon when alone, and

---

58 *The Praise of Musicke*, 151.

59 Ames, *Conscience*, ch. 19, 'Of Singing,' 43.

60 Harris, 'The Excellence of the Duty of Singing' in *Practical Discourses of Singing*, 74.

61 Reynolds, 'Objections considered against the Duty of Singing,' ibid., 113.

62 Newman, 'Directions for the right Performance of the Duty of Singing,' ibid., 170.

63 Lancelot Andrewes, *The Private Devotions of the right Reverend Father in God Lancelot Andrewes* (London, 1647), 82.

sing over to themselves. This may sometimes give their thoughts a divine Turn, and raise a young Meditation.[64]

In this way singing became heralded as an auxiliary to reason during an intensely cerebral age. Its connection to the imagination is perhaps more obvious. What did the imagination signify to English Protestants in the early modern period? They believed it capable of conceiving the most noble and lofty phantasms—but they also believed it to be a weak sister of sorts among the faculties, one unfortunately susceptible to the direct blandishments of the devil. Nevertheless, they respected its power, and the popular connection between the imagination and vocal music enhanced the prestige of singing all the more within the culture.[65]

The Role of Imagination

Imagination played an operative role in Anglican and Puritan schemes of meditation, for an imagination properly reigned in by a holy mind-set was believed finally free to assert its dominance over other faculties. Reynoldes writes, 'I take … Memory and Fancy, or Imagination, to have a more excellent degree of perfection in man, as being indeed the principal Store-houses and treasuries of the operations of the Soul.'[66] During meditation the imagination furnishes the understanding with invention, a 'variety of objects whereon to work,' and thereby

> Quickens and raises the Mind with a kind of heat and rapture proportionable in the inferior part of the Soul, to that which in the superior, Philosophers call Ecstasy; whereby it is possessed with such a strong delight in its proper object, as makes the motions thereof towards it, to be restless and impatient.[67]

Reynoldes concludes that the fancy, or imagination—one's own, and also that of others—is the 'fountain of delight' that raises the mind with 'heat' (i.e., full involvement of the passions) to rapture. He calls this rapture in the

---

64 Isaac Watts, *Divine Songs, Attempted in Easy Language for the use of Children* (London, 1715), preface.
65 Alexander Shapiro and Jeremy Gregory argue that the preservation of Christian orthodoxy was an important impetus for English artistic activity in the late seventeenth and early eighteenth centuries (when sacred poetry and music became favorite causes); Gregory notes that promotion of the arts was especially strategic for the established Anglican church, which was becoming vulnerable to secularism and a growing religious pluralism. For more on the relationship between English Protestantism and the arts during this period, see Gregory and Jeremy Black, *Politics and Society in Britain 1660-1800*; also Shapiro, 'Drama of an Infinitely Superior Nature: Handel's Early English Oratorios and the Religious Sublime,' *Music and Letters* 74 (May 1993): 215-245.
66 Reynoldes, *Treatise of the Passions*, 13.
67 Ibid., 18.

higher soul, ecstasy; in the lower soul, earthly delight.[68] In *The Soules Conflict with it Selfe* Sibbes calls imagination the 'first wheel of the soul':

> If that move amiss, it stirs all the inferiour wheels amiss with it; it stirs itself, and other powers of the soul are stirred by its motions; and therefore the well-ordering of this is of the greater consequence; For as the imagination conceiveth, so usually the judgment concludeth, the will choseth, the affections and carried, and the members execute.[69]

He warns that the imagination, if ungoverned, may become 'a wild and ranging thing,' by allowing the lower parts of the soul to gain control over the superior faculties, and also by creating contrary worlds where evil becomes good, and good, evil: a usurption 'which cannot but breed an unquiet and an unsettled soul.'[70] But Christians gain mastery over this fickle instrument when they embrace biblical truth, and, in so doing, simultaneously find their capacity for emotional experience enlarged: 'Love is an affection full of inventions, and sets the wit a-work to devise good things.'[71]

Sibbes and Reynoldes consider the imagination invaluable for making things pleasing or displeasing to 'the outward man'—although they find it a poor guide for making moral judgments. Far from taking an anti-imaginative stance (as is commonly supposed), they and other early English Protestant divines actually had great respect for this faculty. Sibbes at one point warns believers to watch lest their outward actions offend the imaginations of others, for 'some are taken off in their affection by a fancy, whereof they can give but little reason; and some are more careless in giving offence in this kind, than stands with that Christian circumspection and mutual respect which we owe one to another.'[72] He adds,

> The putting of lively colours upon common truths hath oft so strong working both upon the fancy, and our will and affections: the spirit is refreshed with fresh things, or old truths refreshed; this made the Preacher seek to find out pleasing and acceptable words; and our Saviour Christ's manner of teaching was by a lively representation to mens' fancies, to teach them heavenly truths in an earthly sensible manner; and indeed what do we see or hear but will yield matter to a holy heart to raise it self higher? ... Here is a large field for our imagination to walk in, not only without hurt, but with a great deal of spiritual gain ... a sanctified fancy will make every creature a ladder to heaven.[73]

---

68 Ibid., 213.
69 Sibbes, *Soules Conflict*, 170.
70 Ibid., 164.
71 Ibid., 168.
72 Ibid., 174.
73 Ibid., 177.

Novices to Christian meditation, such as children and young people, are especially prone to imaginative appeals: 'And because childhood and youth are ages of fancy, therefore it is a good way to instill into the hearts of children betimes, the loving of good, and the shunning of evil, by such like representations as agree with their fancies, as to hate hell under the representation of fire and darkness, &c.'[74]

Reynoldes similarly concludes that use of the imagination is the best way to affect those sensitive people possessed of 'more tender wills.'

> The office of the Imagination to the Will, is to quicken, allure, and sharpen its desire towards some convenient object; for it often cometh to pass, that some plausible Fancy doth more prevail with tender Wills, than a severe and sullen Argument: and hath more powerful insinuations to persuade, than the peremptoriness of Reason hath to command. And the reason hereof is, because liberty being natural unto man's Will, that course must needs most of all gain upon it, which doth offer least force unto its liberty: Which is done rather by an Argument of delight, than of constraint; and best of all, when a rational and convincing Argument is so sweet'ned and tempered, to the delight of the ear, that he shall be content to entertain truth for the very beauty and attire of it; so that you shall not know, whether it were the weight of the Reason that over rul'd, or the elegancy that enticed him ... And therefore, in that great work of men's conversion unto God, he is said to allure them, and to speak comfortably unto them, to beseech, and to persuade them; to set forth Christ to the Soul, as altogether lovely, as the fairest of ten thousand, as the desire of the Nations, as the Riches of the World, that men might be inflamed to love the beauty of Holiness.[75]

Reynoldes acknowledges that reason, although it reigns over all the faculties, can seem 'severe,' 'sullen,' 'peremptory,' 'rigid,' and a heavy taskmaster. For this reason, he explains, the ancient Greeks and Romans formed societies and encouraged virtue using 'the sweetness of Eloquence' and 'Musical, Poetical, and Mythological persuasions.' Even Holy Scripture uses metaphor and parables in order to teach eternal truths, he adds.[76] So both Sibbes and Reynoldes would agree that the imagination serves as a kind of vacation for the mind, a welcome relief from the tiring duties of cognition.

> They are not exacted to the rigor and strictness of Reason, nor grounded on the severity of Truth, but are ... the Creation of the Fancy, having a kind of delightful liberty in them, wherewith they refresh and do as it were open and unbind the Thoughts, which otherwise, by a continual

---

74 Ibid., 179.
75 Reynoldes, *Treatise of the Passions*, 19.
76 Ibid., 20.

pressure in exacter and more massie [heavy, ponderous] reasoning, would easily tire and despair.[77]

The subliminal idea that singing represents merriment, freedom, even a 'safe' type of metaphysical anarchy, finds reinforcement in period theology. Vocal music was thought to operate on many different levels, engaging the reason by impressing the soul with profound spiritual and moral lessons while simultaneously involving the imagination. But of perhaps greater import was the belief in singing's power over the emotions, or the passions.

The Role of the Affections

The question of right religious affections looms large within the literature. English devotional writers were very interested in exposing, for good or ill, the cozy, private corners of the soul, the habitual frames of mind and heart worn down to a sheen by long and constant use. Believing that 'as a man thinketh, so he is,' they described at length ways the heart could become soft and pliable; and keeping the affections suitably stirred—and, once stirred, properly aligned and focused—became a consuming project to spiritually-minded men and women.

The Saints' Everlasting Rest deals with this topic in great detail. One point which Baxter returns to repeatedly is the idea that effective meditation must involve the entire self, and so must invoke the cooperation of the affections and the imagination as well as reason: it is 'the acting of all the powers of the soul.' He contrasts meditation (an intensive exercise) with a 'mere employment of the brain' (the type of cogitation students employ in studying for a test, for example). 'It is not bare thinking that I mean, nor the mere use of invention or memory, but a business of a higher and more excellent nature.' Hence, the passions are intimately involved in the process of belief:

> When truth is apprehended only as truth, this is but an unsavoury and loose apprehension; but when it is apprehended as good, as well as true, this is a fast and delightful apprehension. As a man is not so prone to live according to the truth he knows, except it do deeply affect him, so neither doth his soul enjoy its sweetness, except speculation do pass to affection.

He follows this with a central passage concerning the role of the affections in Christian faith:

> The understanding is not the whole soul, and therefore cannot do the whole work. As God hath made several parts in man to perform their several offices for his nourishing and life, so hath he ordained the faculties of the soul to perform their several offices for his spiritual life … the understanding must take in truths, and prepare them for the will, and it

---

77 Ibid.

must receive them, and commend them to the affections. The best digestion is in the bottom of the stomach; the affections are, as it were, the bottom of the soul; and therefore the best digestion is there. While truth is but a speculation swimming in the brain, the soul hath not half received it, nor taken fast hold of it: Christ and heaven have various excellences, and therefore God hath formed the soul with a power of apprehending diverse ways, that so we might be capable of enjoying those diverse excellencies in Christ.

Baxter continues on to call the affections the 'senses of the soul,' by proximity linking the affections to the senses (in faculty psychology the passions are located in the region of the 'sensitive soul,' and thus humans share the ability to emote with other animals).

Even as the creatures having their several uses, God hath given us several senses, that so we might enjoy the delights of them all. What the better had we been for the pleasant, odoriferous flowers and perfumes, if we had not possessed the sense of smelling? or what good would language or music have done us, if God had not given us the sense of hearing? or what delight should we have found in meats, or drinks, or sweetest things, if we had been deprived of the sense of tasting? So also, what good could all the glory of heaven have done us; or what pleasure should we have had, even in the goodness and perfection of God himself; if we had been without the affections of love and joy, whereby we are capable of being delighted in that goodness? And what benefit of strength or sweetness canst thou possibly receive by thy meditations on eternity, while thou dost not exercise those affection which are the senses of the soul, by which it must receive this sweetness and strength?[78]

These excerpts from *The Saints' Everlasting Rest* represent the core of Baxter's devotional thought, indeed quite possibly that of this entire body of English devotional literature. What a soul loves, it grows to resemble. All of these churchmen's belief in predestination and God's sovereignty—doctrines which, on the face of them, would seem to eliminate any interest in the actions of a puny, weak humanity—did not preclude them from making the observation, simple in its obviousness, that a person must see some winsome qualities in Christianity in order to ever be first attracted to it. 'Affection holdeth its object faster than bare judgment doth.'[79] The affections thus play a vital role in both conversion and the ensuing process of sanctification. God did not make the emotions in vain, urges Baxter:

Reason is a sleepy half-useless thing, till some Passion excite it: and Learning to a man asleep is no better for that time than Ignorance. And

---

78 Baxter, *The Saints' Everlasting Rest*, 551.
79 Ibid., 654.

God usually beginneth the awakening of Reason, and the conversion of Sinners, by the awakening of their useful Passions, their Fear, their Grief, Repentance, Desire, &c. I confess, when God awakeneth in me those Passions which I account rational and holy, I am so far from condemning them, that I think I was half a Fool before, and have small comfort in sleepy Reason. Lay by all the passionate part of Love and Joy, and it will be hard to have any pleasant thoughts of Heaven.[80]

English Reformed theologians believed that the affections are involved in conversion and sanctification through a circular pattern, in which emotion both initiates and reinforces desired states of mind. Within this framework, God works on the called individual in various ways; but in the end that person will always experience three emotions in particular:

1) an intense desire for goodness
2) a deep conviction of unworthiness
3) fear of divine judgment

Hearing and believing the Christian offer of forgiveness of sins through Christ, the new convert grows to love God in ever increasing measure. At this point, meditation, singing, and other devotional aids work upon the affections as the outward life becomes visibly transformed; and, in the end, mystically 'possessing Christ,' and reassured that he is similarly 'possessed *by* Christ,' the believer's capacity for love towards God and others is enlarged: he now has the 'tender heart' so prized by devotional writers. English readers were constantly reminded to look inward and consider whether or not their spiritual experiences followed this pattern: if lacking these markers, they ran the danger of practising an illusory 'formal religion' which would only lead to hell. For, 'that knowledge is only saving knowledge, that works the heart to a love, to a joy, and delight, that works the whole man to practise, and obedience; that is only spiritual knowledge.'[81]

In his popular treatise, *The Soules Conflict with it Selfe*, Sibbes refers to the affections as the motions or 'winds' of the soul, terms which theorists of the time also used to describe music—as William Holder wrote, 'All sound is made by Motion, *viz.* by Percussion with Collision of the Air.'[82] Throughout this book, Sibbes represents the soul as a malleable substance, which may be observed and taken into hand in order to be chided, consoled, or challenged, whatever the need might be. Noting that self-scrutiny is 'a course without glory and ostentation in the world,' he calls it 'Both good in

---

80 Richard Baxter, *Poetical Fragments: Heart-Imployment with God and It Self* (London, 1681), preface.
81 Sibbes, *Light from Heaven*, 48.
82 William Holder, *A Treatise of the Natural Grounds, and Principles of Harmony* (London, 1694), 1.

it self, and makes the soul good. For by this means the judgment is exercised and rectified, the will and affections ordered, the whole man put into an holy frame fit for every good action ... by this the soul it self is set in tune, whence there is a pleasant harmony in our whole conversation.'[83]

According to Sibbes, it is to the soul's shame that 'so nimble and swift a spirit ... should be skillful in the story of all times and places, and yet ignorant of the story of it self.'[84] This goal of intensive self-scrutiny easily blends into the personalized singing tradition described in chapter two. And what Sibbes holds up as the ideal is, above all else, an *active* soul. God is pure act, he writes; and the closer the human spirit draws near to him, the more active it necessarily becomes. What is definitely *not* wanted in this picture is a stagnant soul—i.e., one unmoved by the turbulence of holy affections.

> It is not so much the having of grace, as grace in exercise, that preserves the soul; therefore we should ... stir up the grace of God in us, that so it may be kept a working and in vigour and strength ... The soul without action, is like an instrument not played upon, or like a ship always in the Haven. Motion is a preservative of the purity of things.[85]

Singing's ability to stimulate the passions, especially its skill in lifting the spirits to positive emotions of joy and love, borders closely upon the emotional dynamic laid out here. Like other seventeenth-century English Protestants, Sibbes was convinced that it takes actual 'holy violence' to lift the fallen soul from its natural spiral downwards into dullness and melancholy; and, to the period mind, what better antidote to melancholy existed than singing? Although a personal sense of grief and repentance was deemed necessary in the sinner, persistent sorrow was believed to actually harm and weaken the spirit. For joy is the proper temper of the soul, and the most productive: 'the soul never worketh better, than when it is raised up by some strong and sweet affection.'[86] Sibbes calls joy 'the constant temper which the soul should be in.' In *A Treatise of the Passions and Faculties of the Soul of Man*, Reynoldes describes its effect upon the soul:

> [An effect] of Joy is Opening and Dilatation of the heart and countenance, expressing the serenity of the mind, whence it hath the name of *Latitia*, as it were a broad and spreading passion. Now the reason of this motion occasioned by Joy, is the natural desire, which man hath to be united to the thing wherein he delights to make way and passage for its entrance into him. And hence we find in this Passion an exultation and egress of

---

83 Sibbes, *Soules Conflict*, 104.
84 Ibid., 114.
85 Ibid., 223.
86 Ibid., 123.

the spirits, discovering a kind of looseness of Nature in her security, doing many things not out of resolution, but instinct and power transporting both mind and body to sudden and unpremeditated expression of its own content: For of all Passions Joys can be the least dissembled or suppressed ... it exerciseth a kind of welcome violence and tyranny upon a man, as we see in David's dancing before the Ark; and the lame man's walking, and leaping, and praising God, after he had been cured of his lameness.[87]

While a season of grief might be appropriate for a time, Sibbes believes that it should be passed through as quickly as possible in order to return to the more normative happiness. Praise is the best defense against sin, for gratitude can come only from a posture of thankfulness and humility: conversely, sin in the heart seals the lips and stops the voice.[88] The highest possible joy for the Christian is praise, which becomes synonymous with singing. As period writings deem joy the most violent emotion, singing thus represents a tumultuous emotional act. It also represents medicine to the soul: 'How do all creatures praise God, but by our mouths? It is a debt always owing, and always paying; and the more we pay, the more we shall owe; upon the due discharge of this debt, the soul will find much peace.'[89]

Sibbes continues on to call the highest possible strain of the affections *zeal*, 'a seeming distemper,' but actually a most desirable condition: 'It is the glory of a Christian to be carried with full sail, and as it were with a spring-tide of affection. So long as the stream of affection runneth in the due channel, and if there be great occasions for great motions, then it is fit the affections should rise higher, as to burn with zeal ...'[90] Zeal is a focus in *A Treatise of the Affections* as well, where William Fenner lays out his scheme of the nine degrees of spiritual affection. The first six steps, which Fenner calls common to all people, range from complete coldness of heart towards spiritual things to the first, faint stirrings of religious interest. Stages six through nine describe progressive degrees of intensity which are unique to the regenerate. In conversion, step six, 'the affection may be wrought on so far, that the heart is quite overturned from that it was before.'[91] Being 'overturned' implies action from some outside force (God), and also signifies motion and a general excitement. In step seven, 'the heart be engaged for God, as a future wife's heart is set on her fiancee': recovered from its initial upset, the soul grows in love with the life of holiness, just as a young woman's affection for her betrothed deepens. Finally, in the last (and best) stage a soul can reach, 'the heart may be quite

---

87 Reynoldes, *Treatise of the Passions*, 216.
88 Sibbes, *Soules Conflict*, 405.
89 Ibid., 413.
90 Ibid., 96.
91 Fenner, *A Treatise of the Affections*, 23.

given up to the thing which it affects'[92]—it has reached the state of zeal, an extremity of the affections which, according to Fenner, is due to God alone. Zeal is thus the religious part of the soul's passions, and 'a high strain of all the affections, whereby the heart puts forth all its affections with might upon that which it absolutely affects.' It 'most spendeth the spirits ... most busieth the body.'[93] Unlike the medieval scholastic Bonaventura (who defines zeal as the highest degree of love) and the Renaissance humanist Ludovicus Vives (who regards it a combination of indignation and pity), Fenner defines zeal as the intense measure of *all* the affections.

So taken were Anglican and Puritan divines with this concept of zeal that it became a recurring theme throughout the devotional literature. John Preston remarks that prayer is acceptable to God only when it comes from the whole soul, when the thoughts and affections are collected together 'as the lines in the center, or as the Sun beams in a burning Glass, and that makes prayer to be hot and fervent.' Lacking this degree of intensity, prayer remains 'but a cold and dissipated thing, that hath no strength or efficacy in it.'[94] And Baxter cries, 'Keep close to this reviving fire [meditation], and see if thy affections will not be warm.'[95]

The picture of the soul's operations we get from these sources is a complex one which does justice to Sibbes' 'all the turnings and windings and byways of our souls.' A sanctified reason overlooks a smooth moderation of all of the faculties, a pliant imagination, and an underlying emotional intensity and depth of feeling liable to bubble into high pitch whenever the occasion warrants—a type of contained chaos, if you will. Baxter had good reason to call meditation a 'winding up of thy affections to heaven.' The affections were so important to the English Reformed world-view because they occupied prime territory in the landscape of the soul. The passions play a decisive role in drawing a soul to God, and, after conversion, continue to guide the course of sanctification, as the believer falls in love anew with creation, with others, and (most importantly) with God himself. Correspondingly, the subject of the voice's power over such passions represented no small matter to this devotional culture; indeed, singing played a central role within this dynamic, for it affects the sacred and profane passions while simultaneously delighting the imagination.

English divines often mentioned the motions of music in close proximity with the motions of the soul. The title *The Soules Conflict with it Selfe* implies to what extent self-scrutiny became a preoccupation, and Sibbes models a fairly sophisticated level of it, advising his readers, for example, to discern whether their level of grief over sin is becoming morbidly

---

92 Ibid., 23.
93 Ibid., 178, 185.
94 Preston, *The Saints' Daily Exercise*, 7.
95 Baxter, *The Saints' Everlasting Rest*, 498.

excessive. At the same time, singing was believed one of the best agents for regulating the soul's homeostasis. The Presbyterian clergyman John Newman remarks, 'We shall be most affected when what we sing is suited to our Condition, and is expressive of the inward Sense and Language of our Hearts.' He agrees with Sibbes that proper self-diagnosis is essential:

> Christians should consider what special Graces they have more than ordinary need to have exercised and increased, what Corruptions to be mortified and kept under, what Difficulties, and Temptations, and Afflictions they are called to contend and grapple with. Such things as these must direct them both in the matter of their Prayers and Singing, when the choice is left to themselves.[96]

Newman infers that this level of discernment is an advanced spiritual skill. Most tellingly, he next juxtaposes the 'melody of the heart' with singing:

> As in vocal Music, every Note must be sung in its proper Place and Order, and there must be a skillful mixture of them, or there will be no external Melody: so there must be a sweet mixture of every Grace, and a seasonable acting of them upon God, or else there will be no Melody in the Heart. It is a great part of holy Christian Wisdom, to know how to live in the suitable Exercise of Grace, and not to be acting one Grace, when God by his Word of Providence calls for another. It is a great fault in some serious Christians, that they too much indulge themselves in Fear, Sorrow, Grief, etc., whilst they neglect or seldom stir up the nobler Graces of Faith, Love, and Hope and Delight in God; tho' these latter may be more suitable and congruous to their present circumstances, and the Duties they are engaged in.[97]

In all of this we see singing becoming a concrete form of what Puritan and Anglican divines would call 'acting a grace.' As singing combines the intellect with the affections, the imagination, and the body, it implies an archetypal wholeness which the writers acknowledge is one of the greatest benefits of singing. 'Human Nature is fitted to this work [singing] with special Design. The Faculties of Inquiry, Meditation, Delight and Wonder, are to relish the Perfection and Bounties of God, what he is in himself, and what he has done for us; and the tongue is our Glory, that we may sing Praise,' notes Thomas Bradbury.[98] William Harris concludes, ' 'Tis the Exercise of the whole Man. It employs the Facultys and Members of Soul and Body. It engages the full Strength of Nature.'[99]

---

96 Newman, 'Directions for the right Performance of the Duty of Singing' in *Practical Discourses of Singing*, 159.

97 Ibid., 173.

98 Bradbury, 'Arguments for the Duty of Singing,' ibid., 33.

99 Harris, 'The Excellence of the Duty of Singing,' ibid., 64.

The Voice in Active Contemplation

Not only was singing believed to exert a strong influence upon the three faculties most directly involved with meditation—reason, the imagination, and the affections—but the Protestant models contain allusions which point to an even closer symbolic fusion between, on one hand, the outward, physical, and musical voice; and on the other, the inward, invisible and silent operations of the soul. We find many such inferences in the writings of Joseph Hall. Earlier we mentioned his route for the 'digestion' of scriptural truths by the soul: the ear initiates the process by paying attention to the word, the brain does it duty by meditating upon it, then the heart responds emotionally. Next, this message goes to the tongue, which performs the spiritual duties of 'conference' and 'holy confession'; finally, the hand completes the cycle with action. In other words, the path to sanctification culminates in some type of personal, vocal articulation of those divine truths which have been received.

Edmund Calamy also gives the voice a prominent place in his scheme. 'Meditation must enter into three doors, or else it will never do you any good,' he urges.

> 1. It must get into the door of the understanding, and there it is seated, there is the proper place of meditation; but if it rest there, thou art never the better for it.
>
> 2. It must get into the door of thy heart, and of thy affections; and thou must never leave meditating till it get into that door likewise.
>
> 3. The door of thy conversation; for thy meditation must not rest in the affections, but it must likewise have influence into thy conversation, to make thy conversation more holy; thou must so meditate of God as to walk as God walks; and so to meditate of Christ as to prize him, and live in obedience to him.[100]

This stress upon proving, strengthening, and confirming one's spiritual experiences through vocal articulation is a common theme. Early English Protestants believed that the soul which has the mark of God upon it will naturally express itself—and that there is something suspect about one which does not. As John Preston observes, 'You shall find this to be the property of love, he that loveth is very ready to speak of the party loved; love is full of loquacity, it is ready to fall into the praises of the party beloved, and to keep no measure in it, to abound in it, that is the disposition of every man that loveth.'[101]

In other words, no silent and secretive disciples, no cowardly Peter lurking by the fire while his Lord is being scourged, need apply! Christian believers at the same time must also prove their words by their actions: if

---

100 Edmund Calamy, *The Art of Divine Meditation* (London, 1680), 28.
101 John Preston, *The Breast-Plate of Faith and Love* (London, 1630), 75.

they do not, they are merely 'formal discoursers' or 'fashionable auditors'—and divines penned numerous warnings against the perils of religious hypocrisy. The ideal type of vocal expression is thus sincere; it comes from the heart, the inner core of one's being, and is inevitably borne out by one's actions. It will also be fervent: Fenner rebuffs, 'it is a disgrace for Mercy to be begged frigidly ... What makest thou of the mercy of God? Dost thou think that it is not worth a *groan*?'[102]

As if there is a direct pathway between the two, the heart and tongue are closely associated. Dingley writes, 'strong desires and affections, break out in passionate and melting expressions: For the tongue is the heart's interpreter, and out of the abundance within the mouth speaketh.'[103] Reynoldes connects inward and outward elements as well, calling speech 'the Gate of the Soul' and 'the Interpreter of the Conceits and Cogitations of the mind':

> The uses whereof are to convey and communicate the conceptions of the mind (and by that means to preserve humane society) to derive knowledge to maintain mutual love and supplies; to multiply our Delights, to mitigate and unload our sorrows; but above all, to Honour God, and to edify one another, in which respect our Tongue is called our Glory. The force & power of Speech upon the minds of men, is almost beyond its power to express, How suddenly it can inflame, excite, allay, comfort, mollify, transport, and carry Captive the Affections of men.[104]

One of the most intriguing aspects of this contemplative tradition was a technique which utilized vocal terminology and addressed a central problem facing believers. By now we know something of this society's interest in the individual's spiritual condition and life of the soul. What the pious Anglican and Puritan found was a psychic battle raging within. For while the regenerate Christian is a new creation—no longer a slave to sin's power, his life is set on a completely different course than previously— there remains on earth a lingering presence of the old flesh: as Paul laments in Romans: 'The good that I would I do not: but the evil which I would not, that I do.' This conflict lies at the crux of Protestant meditation's dynamic nature. Aware of this battle, Sibbes wrote of the soul's vicissitudes and Baxter modeled in *The Saints' Everlasting Rest* a contemplative method of inner conversation, or dialogue, with the soul which he and other divines called 'soliloquy.'

Upon close examination, Baxter's technique reveals his cohesiveness of vision. The rational faculty starts by calling to mind God's goodness and past providences and remembering all 'the former testimonies of the

---

102 William Fenner, *The Efficacy of Importunate Prayer* (London, 1657), 168.
103 Dingley, *Spirituall Taste*, 29.
104 Reynoldes, *Treatise of the Passions*, 506.

Spirit.'[105] Next, 'this fire in thy breast begins to kindle,' as the emotions become stirred: 'as gazing upon the dusty beauty of flesh doth kindle the fire of carnal love; so this gazing on the glory and goodness of the Lord will kindle this spiritual love in thy soul.'[106] But beyond this arousal lies another step towards the goal of true understanding: the personal stake a soul takes in this knowledge. This is soliloquy, 'pleading the case with our own souls,' where the inner voice preaches to oneself in much the same way that a minister preaches to a congregation.

> As in preaching to others, the bare propounding and opening of truths and duties, doth seldom find that success as the lively application; so it is also in meditating and propounding truths to ourselves. The moving, pathetical pleadings with a sinner, will make him deeply affected with a common truth, which before, though he knew it, yet it never stirred him.[107]

This 'preaching of heaven to the heart' was a powerful application of truth upon the personal conscience. Baxter advises using all the weapons from the rhetorical arsenal in this struggle: 'Enter into a serious debate with it; plead with it in the most moving and affecting language; urge it with the most weighty and powerful arguments: this soliloquy, or self-conference, hath been the practice of the holy men of God in all times.'[108] He reasons,

> Doth not God command thee to teach [the Scriptures] diligently to thy children; and to talk of them when thou sittest in thy house, when thou walkest by the way, when thou liest down, and when thou risest up? And if thou must be skilled to teach thy children, much more to teach thyself; and if thou canst talk of them to others, why not also to thine own heart?[109]

By borrowing the following techniques of oratory, every good Christian can become a preacher to his or her own self:

   1) explication: explaining the biblical truth or doctrine being considered
   2) confirmation: re-emphasizing personal belief in that truth
   3) application: connecting the concept to one's own personal condition

According to Baxter, this process accomplishes many things: it corrects errors in thinking, brings to mind one's duties and obligations, helps us look into the 'soul's mirror' more directly and reprove ourselves for any failings ('chide thy heart for its omissions and commissions, and do it

---

105 Baxter, *The Saints' Everlasting Rest*, 578.
106 Ibid., 580.
107 Ibid., 592.
108 Ibid., 594.
109 Ibid., 596.

sharply till it feel the smart'), and, in the end, brings encouragement and the resolve to be faithful in the future.[110] Soliloquy should be accompanied by an especially intense pitch of emotion:

> Take thy heart as to the brink of the bottomless pit; force it to look in; threaten thyself with the threatenings of the word; tell it of the torments that it draweth upon itself; tell it what joys it is madly rejecting; force it to promise thee to do so no more, and that not with a cold and heartless promise, but earnestly with most solemn asseverations and engagements.[111]

In this way Baxter, like Sibbes, presents a method of meditation which uses the concept of 'holy violence' to improve the soul. The voice serves as both the instigator and relayer of this cleansing spiritual turbulence.

Baxter further counsels his readers to add to their soliloquies what he calls 'ejaculations,' sudden and spontaneous pleas for mercy, joyful outbursts, inarticulate groans, etc. Although these expressions may be either spoken or silent, the impulse remains verbal, as the supplicant imagines physical speech and feels a type of vicarious bodily response while experiencing certain emotions. Again reason, imagination, and the affections unite with the body, through the agency of the voice, to touch upon the transcendent in a powerful way. Baxter promises that those who practice the art of ejaculatory prayer give their souls the best medicine of all.

> The apostle bids us to speak to ourselves in psalms and hymns; and no doubt we may also speak to God in them: this keeps the soul in mind of the divine presence, it tends also exceedingly to quicken and raise it; so that as God is the highest object of our thoughts, so our viewing of him, and our speaking to him, and pleading with him, doth more elevate the soul, and actuate the affections, than any other part of meditation can do ... The men of God, both former and latter, who have left their meditations on record for our view, have thus intermixed soliloquy and prayer; sometimes speaking to their own hearts, and sometimes turning their speech to God: and though this may seem an indifferent thing, yet I conceive it very suitable and necessary *and that it is the highest step that we can advance to in the work.* [Emphasis added.][112]

Other Protestant divines refer to soliloquy, dialogue, and ejaculatory prayer as well. Sibbes maintains that the discipline of inner soliloquy keeps the mind from error:

---

110 Ibid., 593.
111 Ibid., 594.
112 Ibid., 596.

Here therefore is a special use of these Soliloquies, to awake the soul, and to stir up reason cast asleep by Satan's charms, that so scattering the clouds through which things seem otherwise than they are, we may discern and judge of things according to their true and constant nature.[113]

The Crums of Comfort recommends that such 'short desires of the heart, lifted up to God with great fervency' be used at all times, in addition to the prayer book formulas.[114] Arthur Bedford juxtaposes this technique with singing in *The Great Abuse of Music*, where he advises Christian singers to follow the examples of the Psalms: 'From such pious Ejaculations as are in the Psalms being often repeated and sung, do proceed suitable Affections.'[115] Finally, Joseph Hall recommends using ejaculatory prayer in conjunction with the contemplative practice of 'reading the creatures.'

Now as these many monitors both outward and inward, must elevate our hearts very frequently, to God; so those raised hearts must not entertain him with a dumb contemplation, but must speak to him in the language of spirits: All occasions therefore must be taken of sending forth pious and heavenly ejaculations to God; The devout soul may do this more than a hundred times a day, without any hinderance to his special vocation: The Housewife at her Wheel, the Weaver at his Loom, the Husbandman at his Plough, the Artificer in his Shop, the Traveller in his way, the Merchant in his Warehouses may thus enjoy God in his busiest employments; for, the soul of man is a nimble spirit; and the language of thoughts needs not take up time; and though we now, for example's sake, clothe them in words, yet in our practice we need not ... [116]

In sum, this was a devotional culture in which matters of the voice predominated on many levels: sociological, ideological, literal and symbolic. The era's wealth of liturgical and para-liturgical song can now be seen as a manifestation of this tendency. For the devout Anglican and Puritan, speaking and singing gospel truths made them become somehow more alive, as the voice became the supreme organizing principle for matters of the soul. While to be a loquacious Christian was thus deemed a good thing within the spiritual arena, this very ideal ironically became a point of scorn in the broader culture as well. It is, after all, the absurd talkativeness of Zeal-of-the-Land Busy, when he denounces a seller's display of gingerbread as an 'idolatrous grove of images, this flasket of idols,' which lands him into trouble in Jonson's satire *Bartholmew Fair*. The path of those who refuse to remain silent on matters of principle is ever difficult.

---

113 Sibbes, *Soules Conflict*, 197.
114 Michael Sparke, *The Crums of Comfort, with Godly Prayers* (London, 1628), n.p.
115 Bedford, *The Great Abuse of Music*, 230.
116 Joseph Hall, *The Devout Soul*, 27.

Chapter Four

'This Sacred Sensualitie'

'The soul is active, and will be doing, and there is nothing that it is more
naturally inclined to, than delight.'
—Richard Baxter, *Right Rejoycing*

'It is the principal design of the Devil, to hide the Goodness and
Pleasantness of Religion from you: and to make it appear to you as a terrible
or tedious life.'
—Baxter, *A Christian Directory*

'Religion, however mistaken or misrepresented by some, is the most
entertaining thing in nature.'
—Nicholas Brady, *Church Musick Vindicated*

While we know that the idea of spiritual ecstasy exists, both in historical
practice and in contemporary cultures, its precise nature is often left
unexplored, relegated to the hazy annals of mysticism. In examining the
correlations in early modern devotional thought between singing and
sensual pleasure, this chapter will broach this elusive subject and, in so
doing, cast doubt upon the view that early English Protestantism, especially
to the degree that it was tainted by continental Calvinism, was a religion
defined by a masochistic degree of self-loathing and lacking any positive
spiritual elements. On the contrary, anyone who takes the time to read this
prose, with its appealing use of sensual imagery, gains a much different
impression of the culture's piety. Even those somber divines at
Westminster—hardly a rakish lot—answered the mystery of ultimate
purpose with the words 'To glorify God and enjoy him forever.'

Within early English Protestant conception, the act of singing plays a
central role in both the pursuit and realization of this ideal of devotional
pleasure and transcendence. In chapter two, which was concerned with
Protestant logocentrism and its implications upon the era's musical
practice, we focused primarily upon the rational aspects of singing; in
chapter three we discussed the voice's function in the larger operations of
the soul. Now we concentrate on singing's place as a sensual activity, and
the various ways in which vocal music came to embody and express the
visceral self to early modern English culture. William Ames's answer to the
question 'why pray with the voice?' articulated a fundamental hierarchy

within the Anglican and Puritan scheme of things: 'Because God is to be glorified, and to be religiously worshipped by us, not only with our souls, but also with our bodies, and so with our voice.'[1] The voice thus became the emblematic signifier of the body and all that pertains to it.

Although sensuality can imply pain and discomfort—a toothache is also a sensual phenomenon, for example—throughout this literature, and in popular regard, we find the concept primarily linked to pleasure. Alongside their fondness for the Word, English devotional writers were fascinated with the subject of pleasure and its twin, sensuality. Their many sensuous descriptions of the joy of holiness prove that the religious culture of the time did not ignore the existence of sensuality, nor discard its usefulness entirely.[2] While this chapter argues for a 'theology of pleasure' on the part of these divines, it is not my intention to suggest that they were hedonists recklessly trampling upon traditional Christian doctrines of sin and self-denial. Rather, exploring this neglected aspect of the theology may be likened to discovering a forgotten room or dusty attic in an elderly relative's house: an interesting exploration which might yield some family secrets and treasures. By carefully counterbalancing the poles of rationality and sensuality, this literature yields a tightly-configured concept of the voice and presents singing as a highly sensuous activity, both explicitly and by virtue of its place in the context of a literary aesthetic of pleasure in God. In this way the voice serves a unifying function in the perpetual dyad of mind and body.

At the same time that these divines expressed themselves through a sensual literary style, they still took seriously the many biblical admonitions against carnality: as Baxter cautioned, 'take heed of sinking into flesh and earth.'[3] The 'flesh' was an ever-present, dangerously comfortable element, liable to sabotage the unwary at any time. John Owen's definition typifies orthodox Protestant opinion:

> The flesh ... is that inherent corrupt Principle of Depraved Nature, whence all evil Actions do proceed, and wherewith the Actions of all Evil men are vitiated ... the Spirit ... is the holy vital principle of new Obedience wrought in the Souls of Believers by the Holy Ghost, enabling them to live under God.[4]

As the source of all type of human sin, the flesh stands opposed to the activity of the Holy Spirit, the third person of the Trinity, without whose

---

1   Ames, *Conscience*, 2, bk. 4:39.
2   Shakespeare's comedies attest to the fact that early modern England was an earthy age in general, and other writings from the period commonly used such language as well.
3   Baxter, *A Christian Directory*, 173.
4   John Owen, *The Grace and Duty of Being Spiritually-Minded* (London, 1681), 4.

inward presence the life of holiness would not be possible. The flesh (in its negative sense) could also refer to sins of the spirit such as pride and hatred, as well as to the more obviously carnal sins of drunkenness and promiscuity. Conversely, English divines knew that Jesus acknowledged the necessities of the human body, and that this acknowledgement could even be interpreted as bordering, at times, on outright approval of such earthly pleasures as food and wine (for example, the wedding feast at Cana, the gift of costly perfume, and the miracle of the loaves and fishes). Reformed arguments for a married clergy frankly admitted the naturalness of sexual desire and the need for its satisfaction. Thus, early English Protestantism was not synonymous with neo-Platonism in its views of the spirit and the body, and the adjective 'Puritan' is frequently misused as a synonym for 'ascetic' or 'Victorian,' especially in matters involving sexuality. On the contrary, Anglicans and Puritans in the early modern era did not view the body as evil, and the spirit necessarily good; moreover, their eschatology maintained the promise of a sanctified body on earth and a glorified body in the hereafter. This society's interest in domestic life, seen in chapter two, was but one facet of its belief in the possibility of a transcendent spirituality grounded in the human body. To reconcile this dichotomy, this delicate interplay between holiness and satisfaction of the bodily senses, can only be difficult, and these writers appear even to contradict themselves at times with their shifting emphases on steeping oneself in the physical world in order to love God all the more, on one hand, and conversely, on denying oneself and holding onto this life 'lightly' as befits a pilgrim passing through on the road to heaven. However, through the working out of these tensions, these thinkers incidentally reveal further rationale for their culture's fascination with singing and the human voice.

The scheme of the five senses—sight, hearing, smell, taste, and touch—as a *topos* in Western literature extends as far back as Aristotle's *De Anima* and *De Sensu*, and the tradition continued to exert a powerful influence in sixteenth and seventeenth-century England.[5] Like Aristotle, the age believed that the senses represented the gateway to the understanding.[6] Specific allusions to the senses figure prominently in Shakespeare's plays, Elizabethan and Cavalier love poetry, the English metaphysical poets, and

---

5 'The series of five senses was used whenever a writer wanted to speak about perception in its entirety for scientific, moral, religious, erotic, or other purposes.' Louise Vinge, *The Five Senses: Studies in a Literary Tradition* (Lund, Sweden: CWK Gleerup, LiberLaromedel Lund, 1975), 10.

6 'There is nothing in the understanding, but it came into the senses before: and therefore it cannot enter into the heart of man, if it enter not by the eye, or by the ear.' Richard Sibbes, *A Glance of Heaven. Or, a Pretious Taste of a glorious Feast. Wherein thou mayst taste and see those things which God hath prepared for them that love him* (London, 1638), 11.

in Edmund Spencer's allegorical fantasy *The Fairie Queen*. Even a minor writer such as Richard Brathwaite wrote an *Essays Upon the Five Senses* (1620) and gave a sensually evocative title to his devotional anthology *A Spiritual Spicerie* (1638).

English Protestants from this era, with their interest in the realities of the physical body and their use of sensuous language to describe the inner life, were partly following a tradition laid down by ancient and medieval Christian scholars. The early church writers Augustine, Lactantius, and Origen, aware of Aristotle's work on this subject, pondered the question of the bodily senses in an apologetical framework; they in turn influenced the medieval theologians Bonaventura and Aquinas, among others. Augustine's *Confessions*[7] provides an example from the fifth century which drew from the *topos* of the five senses. In book ten, Augustine answers the question 'What is it I love when I love God?' with a description of how the bodily pleasures parallel the inner sensations kindled by devotion, thus introducing the concept of analogous 'senses of the soul':

> It is not the beauty of a body or the glory of the world, not the brightness of the light, this friend of our eyes, not the sweet melodies of songs of all kinds, not the sweet smell of flowers and ointments and spices, not manna and honey, not limbs agreeable for the embracements of the flesh: it is not this that I love, when I love my God. And yet I love a kind of light and a kind of voice and a kind of smell and a kind of food and a kind of embrace, when I love my God, light, voice, smell, food, embrace of my inner man, where that shines for my soul which no room does enclose, and where that resounds which no time does carry off, and where that sells, which no wind does scatter, and where that tastes, which no greediness diminishes, and where that sticks, which no satiety tears away. This is what I love, when I love my God.

Louise Vinge thinks that this passage made a lasting impression upon Christian mystics. It foreshadows later figures such as Meister Eckhart, Teresa of Avila, and St. John of the Cross, all of whom drew upon sensual imagery in order to describe their ecstatic experiences.[8] From the spiritual/material duality of the Incarnation Julian of Norwich inferred: 'For

---

7 Many early English Protestant clergymen knew the *Confessions* in Latin. Its first English translation, *The Confessions of the Incomparable Doctour S. Augustine,* Tobie Mathew, tr. (St. Omer, 1620) was followed by a more explicitly Protestant version, *St. Augustine's Confessions,* William Watts, tr. (London, 1631). An earlier work, Thomas Becon's very popular *The Pomaunder of Prayer* (London, 1560?) also contained excerpts by Augustine.

8 Vinge, *Five Senses*, 41.

I saw full surely that our substance is in God, and also I saw that in our sensuality God is …'[9]

While Protestantism represented a break from the Roman Catholic past, these devotional writers were still educated in a Christian intellectual tradition which had been accumulating since the patristic era. They respected Augustine as a faithful interpreter of Pauline doctrine, quoted Bernard of Clairvaux extensively, and were even known to cite Aquinas (although they had problems with scholasticism's integration of Aristotlean hierarchies into the Christian *schema*). Doubtless they modelled the use of sensual imagery from some of these ancient and medieval sources, as well as from scripture. This acknowledged, similarities between Reformation practice and the Ignatian use of the senses and imagination brings the question of Roman Catholic influence on early English Protestantism to the fore. Anyone familiar with the Counter-Reformation knows something about the abiding impact made by Ignatius of Loyola (1491-1556), the founder of the Jesuits, upon Catholic Europe and the New World. Although an English translation of the *Spiritual Exercises* would not appear until 1736, his ideas did reach England in the seventeenth century through the works of Luis de Granada and Francois de Sales. In the stepwise process known as Ignatian meditation, supplicants are instructed to focus their imagination upon a mystery (such as Christ's crucifixion) or doctrine (such as the existence of heaven) in order to deepen their own devotion. The part of the method most directly involved with the senses is 'the composition of place,' in which an inward, imaginary impression of the scene in question is recreated with the assistance of the five senses. One vivid example is this meditation on Hell from the *Spiritual Exercises*:

> The first point will be to see with the eyes of the imagination those great fires, and the souls as it were in bodies of fire.
>
> The second, to hear with the ears the wailings, the groans, the cries, the blasphemies against Christ our Lord, and against all His saints.
>
> The third, to smell with the sense of smell the smoke, the brimstone, the filth, and the corruption.
>
> The fourth, to taste with the sense of taste bitter things, such as tears, sadness, and the worm of conscience.
>
> The fifth, to feel with the sense of touch how those fires touch and burn the souls.[10]

---

9 Julian of Norwich, *Juliana, anchoret, 1343-1443: A Book of Showings to the Anchoress Julian of Norwich,* Edmund Colledge and James Walsh, eds., (Toronto, 1978), Long Text 55, 2. 566-67. 23-25.

10 Ignatius of Loyola, *Spiritual Exercises*, W.H. Longridge, tr. (London: Robert Scott Roxburghe House, 1919), 67.

It would seem, then, that the integration of sensuality and Christianity was already a well-worn theme by the sixteenth and seventeenth centuries. But I believe that the authors cited throughout this book represent an independent development of this stream of thought. Composition of place was but one feature of the *Spiritual Exercises*, which on the whole presented a distinctly Roman Catholic spirituality that differed in some major points from historic English Protestantism. For this reason its direct influence on these Puritan and Anglican divines remains ambiguous. Under the section 'Rules for thinking with the Church,' for example, one finds such Protestant stumbling blocks as, 'To extol the religious state, and celibacy more than matrimony,' 'To commend the veneration of Relics of the Saints,' 'To commend the building and ornamentation of churches,' and so on. Also prominent are the work's underlying theme of obligatory penance, its detailed structure, and its authoritarian tone—all of which would serve to strengthen the place of the Roman church in the lives of its readers. So while the use of sensuous imagery by Protestant divines can at times resemble Ignatius and other continental sources, the devotional culture we are studying represents, in my opinion, a unique development of Christian spirituality in early modern Europe. To contradict Solomon, there *was* something new under the sun. To ignore the fact that Ignatian spirituality was a movement of great influence and vigor would be to misrepresent history; however, it is a large leap to assume that because Baxter, Preston, Rous, and others employed sensuous imagery in a religious context, and because Ignatius did as well, that must necessarily mean that English Protestants directly copied Roman Catholics in this regard. On the contrary, given the depth of the theological chasm between the two parties during this age, the abiding Reformed horror of the 'anti-Christ' on the papal throne, and the social and political marginalization of Catholic recusants in early modern England, it seems rather that Anglican and Puritan thought on the topic of sensual pleasure was a hybrid which developed in English soil; and (although watered by some ancient and medieval sources in common with continental Catholicism) it thrived in that hyper-controversial age which was early modern England, largely apart from thinkers such as Ignatius—the much-heralded Anglican *via media* notwithstanding.

Aesthetic Principles

Underlying devotional thought on pleasure and sensuality stood the confident view that God is the source of all beauty. This became a favorite subject of popular sermons and devotional works, as well as more specialized treatises on the anatomy of the soul. As John Preston preached before James I:

If ever we saw beauty in the Sun, Moon, Stars, Men, Women, or anything else; all must be more abundantly in God, who is the Maker, Giver, and Author of all these things. For as the worth and value of many pieces of silver is in one piece of gold: so all the petty excellencies, which are scattered abroad in the creatures, are united in God; yea, all the whole Volume of perfections which is spread through Heaven and Earth, is epitomized in him.[11]

While this might seem a matter of course—after all, don't all religions assume that everything good ultimately resides within the object of worship?—the abundance of material on this subject, the creative ways in which this conviction is expressed, and the prominent role it plays in Anglican and Puritan exegesis, are all noteworthy, and suggest that we have neglected an important aspect of English Protestant spirituality—delight— which was crucial in its own day. One common metaphor is that God is an ocean of beauty. Francis Rous promises in *The Heavenly Academie:* 'These drops and dews of grace, by which you are now taught, shall bring you to the sight and fruition of the Teacher himself, who is an ever-flowing fountain, and boundless Ocean of light, wisdom, grace, and glory.'[12] He continues this thought in *The Mysticall Marriage:* 'And God being tasted, overfloweth, and steepeth, and drencheth the soul with overcoming and inebriating sweetness.'[13] And:

Christ Jesus is all lights in one light, all glories in one glory, all beauties in one beauty, all joys in one joy. When he gave light, and glory, and beauty, and joy to the creature, he left the root of light, and glory, and beauty, and joy in himself. So did he leave infinitely more in himself; than he gave out of himself; for an internal and infinite fountain, hath infinitely more in it, than all the streams that ever issued from it: and he is a fountain, for largeness unlimited, and for spring without beginning and ending.[14]

Robert Dingley also calls God 'the Ocean of divine sweetness,'[15] and describes the future bliss of the saints in heaven when they will partake of this abundance:

Christ Jesus is an inexhaustible fountain: there is an unfathomable Ocean of sweetness in God, enough to satisfy thee and all comers. When all the Elect which are a numberless number, shall have tasted divine sweetness

---

11 John Preston, *The Fulnesse of Christ for Us: A Sermon preached at the Court before King James of Blessed Memory* (London, 1640), 9.
12 Rous, *The Heavenly Academie,* 187.
13 Rous, *The Mysticall Marriage,* 46.
14 Ibid., 44.
15 Robert Dingley, *The Spirituall Taste Described and a Glimpse of Christ Discovered,* 43.

here, and drunk their fill of those Crystal Rivers in glory, 'twere blasphemy to think there should be the less in God, still in Christ fullness dwells. The Sun hath not the less for filling all the lesser vessels of the Stars with light ... [16]

Another writer who employed that imagery of God as an infinite sea of goodness was a divine who, like so many others in the seventeenth century, straddled the mainstream Anglican/Puritan divide, Edmund Calamy the elder. He advises:

When thou meetest with a learned man, or a wise man, or a beautiful creature, it is a very excellent meditation to consider, if there be so much beauty, so much wisdom in the creature, O what is there in God, who is the ocean of beauty! If there be so much comeliness, so much excellency here below, Oh what is there above![17]

Richard Baxter had a special affinity for penning ecstatic passages about the beauty of God. When he wrote *The Saints' Everlasting Rest*, destined to become the classic manual of seventeenth-century Protestant meditation, he was seriously ill and believed that he was dying. Perhaps these extreme circumstances account in part for the lucidity of Baxter's vision and the hypnotic quality this vast work often achieves. Throughout the course of his long life (he was to live forty more years), Baxter developed a thoughtful and cogent philosophy on the relationship of pleasure to spirituality. As a Puritan, he was obsessed with the need for personal 'heart-sincerity' in religious belief and practice, seen in his observation that 'though an outward ordinance may delight the ear, or tickle the fancy, yet is is the view of God that must ravish the soul.'[18] God must be loved best above all other suitors. Human attempts to represent holiness and divinity are beautiful inasmuch as they partake of the far greater beauty found in God: 'Though the real presence do afford the choicest joy, yet the presence of its imperfect idea, or image in thy understanding may afford me a great deal of true delight.'[19] Even *unlawful* sensual pleasures, in their own way, point to God (and Baxter admits that they are pleasures, although of the wrong sort): 'Sure, then, there are high delights with God. If the way to hell can afford such pleasure, what are the pleasures of the saints in heaven?'[20] He goes so

---

16 Ibid, 16.
17 Calamy, *The Art of Divine Meditation*, 19. Calamy, a Calvinist Anglican clergyman, is an interesting case in point: never an extreme Puritan, he was eager to see Charles II restored; however, when offered a bishopric at the Restoration, he refused it (along with Baxter), and thereby aligned himself outwardly with Nonconformity at the end of his life. His sons continued on in the Nonconformist tradition.
18 Baxter, *The Saints' Everlasting Rest*, 560.
19 Ibid., 589.
20 Ibid., 601.

far as to identify the taking of pleasure in meditation the true mark of a believer: 'If thy meditation tend to fill thy note-book with notions, and good sayings, concerning God and not thy heart with longings after him, and delight in him, for aught I know thy book is as much a Christian as thou,' he quips.[21] An emphasis upon the necessity of claiming heavenly joy for one's own winds through Baxter's writings like a leitmotif. In *Right Rejoycing* he argues:

> From others we may have joy derivatively at the second hand: but only from God as the Original and first cause ... If God be not to be rejoiced in, the affection of joy is made in vain: for he is goodness itself, and there is nothing lovely or delectable but what is in him. And what is Heaven, but the fruition of God?[22]

Following closely upon the principle that God is the source of all beauty is the corollary that God deserves the love of his creation. To this end, Rous advises: 'Let the pieces and earnests of heavenly joys stir up thy desires and affections, to the fruition of the fullness of joys; let these drops of God's sweetness enflame thy soul with a thirst and longing to enjoy God the fountain of this sweetness.'[23] John Preston recommends that Christians try to love God in some proportion to his infinite perfection and lovableness:

> We should ... answer the fullness of Christ with a fullness of affection fully to believe and trust in him, fully to love and adore him, fully to joy and delight in him. For it is good reason that the affections should be answerable to the Object. A little excellency deserves at our hands a little love and esteem, more excellency more love; but when there is fullness of excellency, we ought to prosecute it with all fullness of affections. All excellency of the creature in comparison of this, is but a drop to the Ocean, and as a spark to the whole element of fire. If therefore we proportion our affections to the object ... we must bestow upon the creature but a drop of love and delight, but the full stream of our affections should run after Christ, in whom is all fullness of perfection.[24]

Joseph Hall, who was fascinated with the relationship between creatures and the Creator, laments that the human species is ungratefully silent compared to the rest of the cosmos:

> Every plant says, look on me, and acknowledge, the life, colour, form, smell, fruit, force that I have from the power of my Creator ... yea the very mute fishes, are in their very silence, vocal, in magnifying the

---

21 Ibid, 553.

22 Richard Baxter, *Right Rejoycing: or, The Nature and Order of Rational and Warrantable Joy* (London, 1660), 15.

23 Rous, *The Mysticall Marriage*, 212.

24 Preston, *The Fulness of Christ for Us*, 8.

infinite wisdom and power of him that made them, and placed them in those watery habitations ... what a shame were it for man, to whom alone God hath given an understanding heart, a nimble tongue, and articulate language, wherein he can express his rational thoughts, to be wanting to this so universal devotion? and to be insensible of the great works of God, as the ground that he treads upon?[25]

The upshot of all this is that in loving the highest possible good, the soul gradually comes to mirror the object of its affections. Sibbes exhorts

The more we set before the soul that quiet estate in heaven, which the souls of perfect men now enjoy, and it self ere long shall enjoy there; the more it will be in love with it, and endeavour to attain unto it. And because the soul never worketh better, than when it is raised up by some strong and sweet affection; let us look upon our nature, as it is in Christ, in whom it is pure, sweet, calm, meek, every way lovely. This sight is a changing sight, love is an affection of imitation, we affect a likeness to him we love. Let us learn of Christ to be humble and meek, and then we shall find rest to our souls. The setting of an excellent idea and platform before us, will raise and draw up our souls higher, and make us sensible of the least moving of spirit, that shall be contrary to that, the attainment whereof we have in our desires. He will hardly attain to mean things, that sets not before him higher perfection.[26]

The third and last principle is the intriguing belief that Christians, besides inheriting the kingdom of God in resurrected and sanctified bodies, will also experience a more vivid and complete type of sensual perception in heaven which earthly senses can only foreshadow. Watts predicts in *The World to Come.*

What new kinds of sensations shall entertain us in that day, what a rich variety of senses we shall enjoy, what well-appointed and immortal organs we shall be furnished with, instead of our present feeble eyes and ears, and what glorious and transporting objects shall surround us in those unknown worlds, and fill the enlarged powers of the soul with sensible as well as intellectual delights![27]

As Robert Bolton succinctly promises: 'Every sense shall be filled with its several singularity and excellency of all possible pleasure, and perfection.'[28]

---

25 Joseph Hall, *Select Thoughts, One Century, also the Breathings of the Devout Soul*, 54.

26 Sibbes, *Soules Conflict*, 123.

27 Watts, *The World to Come*, 508.

28 Robert Bolton, 'Of Heaven,' *Mr. Bolton's Foure Last Things: Death, Judgement, Hell, Heaven*, 141.

Sensory Allusions within the Literature

Keeping these principles in mind: 1) God is the source of infinite goodness, beauty, and truth; 2) it is everyone's joyful duty to love him; and 3) eternity holds the promise of an even better type of sensual perception; it follows that a sensual literary style would prove useful in tracing the implications of these doctrines. For pleasure is primarily recognized through, and transmitted via, the five senses. The figurative language used by Puritans and Anglicans is rich and evocative. For example, Calamy references the sense of smell when he compares meditation to the bruising of spices.

> The reason why the promises of God do no more affect your hearts, when the Saints of God taste no more sweetness in the promises, is because you do not ponder and meditate upon them ... As it is with spices; unless they be bruised, they never smell sweet; and as it is with a Pomander, unless you do rub it, you will never smell the sweetness of it; no more will you ever taste the Heavenly comfort that is in the Promises of the Gospel, unless you rub them, unless you bruise, unless you chew them by meditation.[29]

Sibbes uses similar words: 'As sweet spices yield small savour, until they are beaten to powder, so the wonderful works of God are either, not at all, or very slightly smelt in the nostrils of man who is of dull sense, unless they be rubbed and chafed in the mind, through a fervent affection ...'[30] Baxter instructs: 'Do thou expatiate in the praises of God, and open his excellences to thine own heart, till thou feel the life begin to stir, and the fire in thy breast begin to kindle ... Bruising will make the spices odoriferous, and rubbing the pomander will bring forth the sweetness.'[31]

Imagery of appetite and eating also occurs frequently—and often apart from discussions of holy communion, the expected occasion for such metaphors. Authors from the period commonly associated the sense of taste with the Fall: Brathwaite mentions Eve's apple in his *Essays Upon the Five Senses*. In *The Saints' Everlasting Rest* Baxter couples food with music:

> Having showed thee how thou must set upon this work, I come now to direct thee in the work itself, and to show thee the way which thou must take to perform it. All this has been but to set the instrument (thy heart) in tune, and now we are come to the music itself: all this hath been but to get thee an appetite; it follows now that thou approach unto the feast; that thou sit down and take what is offered, and delight thy soul as with marrow and fatness.[32]

---

29 Calamy, *Art of Divine Meditation,* 33.
30 Sibbes, *Divine Meditations and Holy Contemplations*, preface.
31 Baxter, *The Saints' Everlasting Rest*, 580.
32 Ibid., 570.

English divines liked to describe meditation in terms of a nourishment of spirit akin to the body's digestion of food. Calamy: 'Meditation, while it is in the understanding, chews upon the things of God, and of Christ, and of Heaven, but when the understanding hath chewed these things, it must not devour all these things itself, but it must convey the meat it hath chewed ... into the heart, and into the will, and into the affections, and into the conversation.'[33] Hall: 'The food that is received into the soul by the ear, is afterwards chewed in the mouth thereof by memory, concocted in the stomach by meditation, and dispersed into the parts by conference and practice.'[34] Ussher: 'Set apart some time for Meditation, that the word may be engrafted in thy heart. The Minister indeed he breaks the bread of life, that is it which must beget Grace, yet if it be not digested, it will do thee no good. If the meat that thou eatest be not digested, it will do thee no good. You see the necessity of labour to retain the word, to digest it, to make it thine own, that you may be transformed by it: and as a man's meat is turned into his substance, so the word of God being digested will nourish you.'[35]

We also find the related concepts that 'to know,' in its fullest sense, is to experientially *taste*, and that the regenerate soul has a taste, or special affinity for holiness, all of its own. 'Spiritual life hath answerable taste, and hunger and thirst after spiritual helps,' writes Sibbes.[36] Rous promises that participation in 'the heavenly Academy,' bestows 'knowing by tasting.'[37] Robert Dingley based *The Spirituall Taste Described and a Glimpse of Christ Discovered* on this analogy. According to part one, entitled 'Divine Relishes of matchless Goodness,' understanding spiritual truths requires 1) seeing knowledge, and 2) tasting knowledge: 'As meat in the platter will not nourish us unless we taste it, so here God is full of goodness, but all this will be nothing to you, nay it shall be something against you, unless you taste it, unless by faith you apply it, and have interest in it.'[38] John Owen writes along similar lines that true spiritual-mindedness consists of 1) an exercise of the mind; 2) the inclination of the mind from the affections; and, especially, 3) a relish in spiritual things, which Owen calls *gust*, denoting an especially enthusiastic type of pleasure.

> A Complacency of mind from that Gust, relish and Savour which it finds in spiritual things, from their suitableness unto its constitution, Inclinations and desires. There is a Salt in Spiritual things, whereby they are condited [pickled or preserved]; also, medicine made sweet, and made savoury unto a renewed Mind; though to others they are as the White of

---

33 Calamy, *Art of Divine Meditation,* 28.
34 Hall, *The Devout Soul,* 109.
35 Ussher, *Method for Meditation* ,15.
36 Sibbes, *Soules Conflict,* 5.
37 Rous, *The Heavenly Academie,* 31.
38 Dingley, *Spirituall Taste,* 27.

an Egg, that hath no taste or savour in it. In this Gust and Relish lies the sweetness and satisfaction of spiritual life. Speculative Notions about Spiritual things, when they are alone are dry, sapless and barren. In this Gust we taste by Experience that God is Gracious, and that the Love of Christ is better than Wine, or whatever else hath the most grateful relish unto a sensual Appetite. This is the proper foundation of that Joy which is unspeakable and full of Glory.[39]

But most intriguing is when the sense of taste is linked to singing. Nathaniel Homes asserts in *Gospel Musick*: 'The truth is, devout singing of Psalms is a favorite sauce to relish every condition and ordinance, that is an iterated ordinance … Yea I may say, this spiritual sauce is meat itself.'[40] Cotton Mather writes in *The Accomplished Singer*: 'Christian, in thy Spiritual Songs, which are Fat things full of Marrow, be still Inquisitive, What is there of a Glorious Christ, which I am now led unto the contemplation of? Getting a Taste of that, thou hast the very Marrow of them.'[41] His reference to devotional songs being 'fat things full of marrow' is a rich one which brings to mind the interesting image of 'eating' a song—the idea that singing initiates a metaphorical type of 'digestion' in which the soul gains supernatural knowledge and comfort. Eating is the process which supports physical life, and we have seen how fervently early modern Protestants believed in the power of the Word to nourish life in the Spirit. They knew that the analogy of eating a song was reminiscent of Psalm 119:103: 'How sweet are thy works to my taste, yea sweeter than honey to my mouth'; also, of the voice's command to John in Rev. 10:9 that he 'eat the book.' Mather suggests that believers gain a special level of knowledge through sacred vocal music as the singer enters a type of contemplative state where the sublimity of God may be glimpsed. His excursions into the symbolic function of singing are notable for the extent to which they verge on the extraordinary and supernatural, yet avoid crossing into occult territory, as the fifteenth-century humanist Marcilio Ficino did.[42] Like Mather, Homes also grants the voice a central place in

---

39 Owen, *The Grace and Duty of Being Spiritually-Minded*, 6.
40 Homes, *Gospel Musick*, 8.
41 Mather, *Accomplished Singer*, 18.
42 In the fifteenth century, Ficino wrote in his *De Vita coelitus comparanda*: 'Remember that song is the most powerful imitator of all things. For it imitates the intentions and affections of the soul, and speech, and also reproduces bodily gestures, human movements and moral characters, and imitates and acts everything so powerfully that it immediately provokes both the singer and hearer to imitate and perform the same things,' 138. The Italian humanist's other, more magical speculations, however, certainly never influenced the English devotional culture to the extent of these Anglican and Puritan divines. See D.P. Walker, 'Ficino's *spiritus*

devotion: acknowledging that singing is 'a favorite sauce' which makes meditation all the more enjoyable, he considers it more than gilt on the spiritual lily—it is, rather, the *'meat itself.'* He concludes that singing is a template of the entire Christian experience, with the unique capacity to reflect all its phases: 'In singing we pray, we praise, we confess, we petition, we exhort, we meditate, we believe, we joy, we mourn.'[43]

Does such use of sensual analogies by Anglican and Puritan divines have any bearing upon the sociology of singing we are defining? I believe that it does, for by virtue of its prevalence and strategic position in key passages, the sensuous mode of expression transcended its rhetorical function to contribute to and define popular religious experience of this culture. The use of language plays an important role in formulating a sense of identity for both individuals and groups: consider, for example, the famous French pride in their tongue which has led to official restrictions against English incursions. In a similar way, the sensual orientation of popular devotional literature alludes to certain theological distinctives which filtered down to affect the real, everyday lives of early English Protestants. How did this happen? First, as the senses deal with the realm of perception, the senses also deal with the individual: only one's own personal body can feel pain, enjoy food and wine, smell perfume, etc. In the same way, Protestant doctrine emphasized the personal condition of each soul to such an extent that Puritan autobiographies remain exemplars of an almost obsessive degree of self-scrutiny. This culture viewed the Church as the mystical body of believers, yes, and therefore prized community highly; however, it shone a spotlight onto the individual in a new way. Being born into a generally Christian society would not suffice when it came to eternal salvation. The state of the individual soul became the focus. Second, in using sensuous imagery to describe the life of holiness these writers confirm the Christian eschatological ideal of a sanctified body. God did not create humanity as disembodied spirits: we are born into flesh and blood; Christ was incarnated into flesh and blood; we are sanctified while living in flesh and blood; and heaven holds the promise of a more glorious body yet. Finally, these writers exhibit a measure of common-sense gratitude as well: believing the senses to be, after all, gifts from God, they assumed their proper duty was to use and enjoy them

Baxter *contra* Augustine

The mutual relationship between the outer bodily senses and the inner spiritual life figures prominently with these thinkers. Baxter, in particular,

---

and Music,' in *Music, Spirit and Language in the Renaissance* (London: Variorum Reprints, 1985), pp. 131-150.
43 Homes, *Gospel Musick*, 8.

expounded at great length on the Christian's enjoyment of the body and sensual perception: perhaps something within his temperament found this subject an especially agreeable one. A figure whose biography traversed both sides of the ecclesiastical spectrum and whose works have remained popular for over three centuries, his ideas certainly merit a closer look. A passage from *Reasons for the Christian Religion* serves as a good preface as it reveals the gentle face of Puritan piety:

Doubtless as the soul, while it dwelleth with flesh, doth receive its objects by the mediation of the sense, so God hath purposely put such variety of sensible delicacies into the creatures, that by every sight, and smell, and hearing, and touch, and taste, our souls might receive a report of the Sweetness of God whose goodness all proceed from: and therefore this is the Life which we should labour in continually, to see God's goodness in every lovely sight, and to taste God's goodness in every pleasant taste, and to smell it in every pleasant odour, and to hear it in every lovely word or sound; that the motion may pass on clearly without stop, from the senses to the mind and will, and we may never be so blockish as to gaze on the Glass, and not to see the Image in it; or to gaze on the Image and never consider whose image it is; or to read the book of the Creation, and mark nothing but the words and letters, and never mind the sense and meaning. A philosopher, and yet an atheist or ungodly, is a monster; one that most readeth the book of nature, and least understandeth or feeleth the meaning of it.[44]

In other words, Baxter considers the senses misused when they are viewed as ends in themselves—they must always be enjoyed as indicators of God's goodness and fertile creativity. Just as the Christian needs to put on the spectacles of scripture in order to understand the nature of reality, he also needs to put on the spectacles of sense. Baxter writes more on 'sacred sensuality' in book four of *The Saints' Everlasting Rest*, where he grants the bodily senses the power of the 'strength of the flesh,' plus the advantages of being personal, intimate, and easily discernible.

Why sure it will be a point of our spiritual prudence, and a singular help to the furthering of the work of faith, to call in our sense to its assistance: if we can make us friends of these usual enemies, and make them instruments of raising us to God, which are the usual means of drawing us

---

44 Richard Baxter, *The Reasons of the Christian Religion, The First Part, Of Godliness: Proving by Natural Evidence the Being of God: the Necessity of Holiness, and a future Life of Retribution; the Sinfulness of the World; the Desert of Hell; and what hope of Recovering Mercies intimate. The Second Part, Of Christianity: Proving by Evidence Supernatural and Natural, the certain Truth of the Christian Belief: First meditated for the well-setling of his own Belief; and now published for the benefit of others* (London, 1667), 42.

from God, I think we shall perform a very excellent work ... for God would not have given us either our senses themselves, or their usual objects, if they might not have been serviceable to his own praise, and helps to raise us up to the apprehension of higher things.[45]

He describes how the Word sets the example of utilizing such objects of sense:

It is very considerable, how the Holy Ghost doth condescend in the phrase of Scripture, in bringing things down to the reach of sense; how he sets forth the excellencies of spiritual things in words that are borrowed from the objects of sense; how he describeth the glory of the new Jerusalem, in expressions that might take even with flesh itself ... doubtless if such expressions had not been best, and to us necessary, the Holy Ghost would not have so frequently used them ... as the Spirit doth speak, so we must hear; and if our necessity cause him to condescend in his expressions, it must needs cause us to be low in our conceivings.[46]

For Baxter, a cardinal value of the senses is that they positively allude to spiritual realities and virtues which are otherwise only conceivable by their negative, by what they are not:

Those conceivings and expressions which we have of spirits, and things merely spiritual, they are commonly but second notions, without the first; but mere names that are put into our mouths, without any true conceivings of the things they signify: or our conceivings which we express by those notions or terms, are merely negative; what things are not, rather than what they are: as, when we mention spirits, we mean they are not corporal substances, but what they are we can tell no more than we know what is Aristotle's *Materia Prima*. It is one reason of Christ's assuming and continuing our nature with the Godhead, that we might know him the better, when he is so much nearer to us; and we might have more positive conceivings of him, and so our minds might have familiarity with him, who before was quite beyond our reach.[47]

Baxter continues, 'But what is my scope in all this?' Is it that we should picture Christ 'as the papists do,' through representational art, or do Protestants expect that heaven will be made of literal gold and pearls? No, he disparages such views as idolatrous and warns that they 'would but seduce and drawn down thy heart.'[48] Yet he stands by the conviction that the senses provide the best vehicle, for the time being, for understanding spiritual things: 'Though these be ... drawn from the manner of men, yet

---

45 Baxter, *The Saints' Everlasting Rest*, 598.
46 Ibid.
47 Ibid.
48 Ibid., 600.

there is somewhat in God which we can see no better yet than in this glass, and which we can no better conceive of than in such notions, or else the Holy Ghost would have given us better ... Bring down thy conceivings to the reach of sense.'[49] For men and women find sensual perception comfortable:

> Excellency without familiarity doth more amaze more than delight us; but love and joy are promoted by familiar acquaintance. When we go about to think of God and glory in proper conceivings, without these spectacles we are lost, and have nothing to fix our thoughts upon. We set God and heaven so far from us, that our thoughts are strange, and we look at them as things beyond our reach, and beyond our line, and are ready to say, That which is above is nothing to us: to conceive no more of God and glory, but that we cannot conceive them, and to apprehend no more, but that they are past our apprehension, will produce no more love but this— to acknowledge that they are so far above us that we cannot love them; and no more joy but this—that they are above our rejoicing. And therefore put Christ no farther from you than he hath put himself, lest the Divine nature be again inaccessible.[50]

Now it is interesting that Baxter, with his positive approach to the senses, differs significantly on this point from Augustine (Austin), whom early modern English Protestants otherwise respected and patterned themselves after. The church father was probably influenced on this point by Plotinus and other pagan neoplatonists who taught renunciation of the world and distrust of bodily pleasure.[51] Baxter, on the other hand, came from a culture which pointedly celebrated marriage in contrast to the former celibate hegemony. The contrast between the two theologians is apparent in book ten of the *Confessions*, where Augustine follows the series of the bodily senses as he describes the temptations of the flesh and his struggle to resist them. In reading excerpts like the following—the first concerning his distrust of the pleasures of taste; the second, a famous indictment of vocal music—it is easy to see how this particular facet of Augustine's thought became a model to later centuries of Christian anchorites and ascetics:

> Thou hast taught me this: that I should partake of foods as if they were medicines. But I reach the condition of peaceful satisfaction, passing from the annoyance of need; I am beset in this very transition by the snare of conscupiscence. The transition itself is a sensual delight, yet there is no other way of transition than that which necessity forces us to pass over.

---

49 Ibid., 598.
50 Ibid.
51 According to Colleen McDannell and Bernard Lang, that Augustine tempered his ascetism after this time is apparent in his later work, *City of God.* See McDannell and Lang, *Heaven: A History* (New Haven: Yale University Press, 1988), 54-66.

Since health is the reason for eating and drinking, perilous enjoyment joins its company, like a lackey, and often strives to get in front so as to become the reason for that act which I claim, and wish, to do only for the sake of health.[52]

The pleasures of hearing had held me in tighter bonds and had imposed their yoke upon me, but Thou didst break it and deliver me. I admit that, at present, when Thy words are chanted with sweet and well-trained voice in tones to which those words give life, I do take some little pleasure ... Yet, the bodily delight, which should not be allowed to enervate the mind, often deceives me, when sense does not keep company with reason so as to follow it passively; but, although it owes the fact of its admission to reason, it strives even to run ahead and lead it. So, in these matters I sin without noticing it, but afterwards I become aware of it.[53]

Augustine's suspicion of singing's 'bodily delight ... which often deceives me' contrasts sharply with Baxter's frank enthusiasm about the spiritual potential of the senses evident above. In fact, Baxter pays singing the highest compliment in this glimpse of domestic life from his *Poetical Fragments*:

For myself, I confess that Harmony and Melody are the Pleasure and Elevation of my Soul, and have made a Psalm of Praise in the Holy Assembly, the chief delightful exercise of my Religion and my Life ... It was not the least comfort that I had in the converse of my late dear Wife, that our first in the Morning, and last in Bed at Night, was a Psalm of Praise (till the hearing of others interrupted it). Let those that favour not Melody, leave others to their different Appetites, and be content to be so far Strangers to their Delights.[54]

Chapters 30 through 34 of the *Confessions* contain Augustine's meditations on the five senses, and he does not view them kindly. Baxter parallels this outline in chapter 16 of *The Saints' Everlasting Rest*. Here their difference over the inherent nature of the senses is clearest. Augustine disparages any delight taken in the satisfaction of hunger, and dismisses eating as a symptom of disability and manifestation of man's sinful corruption, since the body needs food to 'repair the daily running down of the body.'[55] But Baxter takes the opportunity to enjoy 'the lawful delights of moderated senses,' and encourages his readers to consider the higher things these sensual manifestations allude to: 'Think with thyself; How sweet is food to my taste when I am hungry, especially ... that which my

---

52 Augustine, *Confessions*, Vernon J. Bourke, tr. (New York: Fathers of the Church, Inc., 1953), 302.
53 Ibid., 307.
54 Baxter, *Poetical Fragments*, preface.
55 Augustine, *Confessions*, 301.

soul loveth, that which my temperature and appetite do incline to! What delight hath the taste in some pleasant fruit, in some well relished meats, and in divers junkets?'[56]

Augustine's tone in chapter 34 of the *Confessions*, where he fears the seductions of sight, rings similarly dour: 'The eyes love beautiful and diverse shapes, brilliant and pleasing colors. Let these things not occupy my soul ... this queen of the colors, this light diffusing all things which we see, wherever I may be throughout the day, flitting about in manifold ways, entices me while doing something else and not noticing her.'[57] This differs sharply from Baxter's treatment: 'How delightful are beauteous sights to the eye, such as curious pictures, sumptuous, adorned, well-contrived buildings, handsome necessary rooms, walks, prospects, gardens stored with variety of beauteous and odoriferous flowers; or pleasant meadows which are natural gardens!'[58]

Baxter must have known the *Confessions* well, because he follows Augustine's line of development and next considers the delights available through natural knowledge and science. Augustine dismisses the human quest for learning as 'a vain and curious desire' and equates it with the biblical 'concupiscence of the eyes.' His suspicious tone—'Behold, in this vast forest filled with pitfalls and perils ...' 'By how many machinations of temptation does the Enemy work with me ...'[59] is foreign to Baxter, who treats scientific investigation in a positive light and invites his readers to consider 'what a pleasure is it to dive into the secrets of nature; to find out the mystery of arts and sciences, to have a clear understanding in logic, physics, metaphysics, music, astronomy, geometry, &c! If we make but any new discovery in one of these, or see a little more than we saw before, what singular pleasure do we find therein!'[60]

So while both Baxter and Augustine would agree that the ultimate end of sensual perception should be the glory of God, Baxter, unlike Augustine, never criticizes the sensory pleasures in themselves. Other Anglican and Puritan divines also differed with Augustine in their appraisal of earthly pleasure. Mather's regard for trained vocalists, for example—'the Skill of Regular Singing, is among the Gifts of God unto the Children of Men, and by no means unthankfully to be Neglected or Despised'[61]—glows in comparison to Augustine's guilty admission of the pleasure he found in music. These discrepancies within the broader Augustinian camp show how we lose a knowledge of theological subtleties to our own disadvantage. For

---

56 Baxter, *The Saints' Everlasting Rest*, 601.
57 Augustine, *Confessions*, 308.
58 Baxter, *The Saints' Everlasting Rest*, 602.
59 Augustine, *Confessions*, ch. 35.
60 Baxter, *The Saints' Everlasting Rest*, 602.
61 Mather, *Accomplished Singer*, 22.

by painting a wide swath, in this case equating the views of early English Protestants with the more ascetic Augustine, we miss an important element of this period which bears significantly upon its conception of singing: its advocacy of innocent sensual pleasures.

Reading the Creatures

A high esteem for the body and the senses also evinced itself within Anglican and Puritan circles through the popular devotional practice of 'reading the creatures.' 'The Book of the Creatures' was one of three interrelated 'books' recognized by English Protestants as sources of spiritual wisdom, the other two being the book of the individual conscience and (supreme over all) the book of the Word, the Bible. They understood the term 'creature' to mean the natural world in all of its diversity: rivers, oceans, sky, trees, flowers, animals, weather, the seasons, the human body, etc., as well as fruits of civilization such as architecture, gardens, wine, poetry, literature, education, painting and music. In essence, all tangible things in life, as well as some intangible ones (such as music and philosophy) were looked upon as creatures, and thus mirrors of God. Calamy's statement is typical:

> You must know, that all the whole Creation is a picture of God; it is God's Looking-glass, wherein you may behold the God of Heaven and Earth; there is no Creature but it hath the Image of God upon it; there is not the least spice of grace but you that are spiritual may read God in it … the book of the Creature is a rare book, wherein a man may learn excellent things concerning Heaven and heavenly things, excellent instructions.[62]

Contrary to being 'so heavenly-minded as to be no earthly good,' the devotional ideal here is to *immerse* oneself into the creatures in order to, paradoxically, rise above them and learn more about God. Preaching neither a total abnegation of the body nor a triumphalist contempt and disregard for nature, this theology rather seeks a heightened awareness of the entire perceptual realm, a process in which the senses play a crucial role. Christians, in fact, enjoy life's pleasures the most, as only believers are capable of exercising this type of spiritual sight completely:

> Herein lies the excellency of a Christian, that he is able to spiritualize natural things … a godly Christian is like a heavenly alchemist, that can draw Heaven out of a Spider as it were; draw something of God out of a Toad, out of a viper, out of any creature of God, much more out of the Heavens, Sun, Moon and Stars.[63]

---

62 Calamy, *Art of Divine Meditation*, 7.
63 Ibid., 15.

Joseph Hall was another divine who wrote extensively on this subject. His *Occasional Meditations* shows how common aspects of seventeenth-century life provided fertile material for reading the creatures. He deems no area of life too trivial, as the range of topics (there are 140 of them in his book) include: 'Upon the Sight of an Eclipse of the Sun,' 'Upon Occasion of a Spider in his Window,' 'Upon the Barking of a Dog,' 'Upon the Hearing of the Street-cries in London,' 'Upon Hearing of Music by Night,' 'Upon the Shutting of One Eye,' 'Upon an Arm Benumbed,' 'Upon the Stinging of a Wasp,' and 'Upon a Medicinal Potion.' Significantly, Hall references all five senses—sight, hearing, touch, taste, and smell—in these miniatures. Viewing his own comfort (sight) contrasted to a robin's nest, he exclaims, 'What a shame is it for me, that see before me so liberal provisions of my God and find myself set warm under my own roof, yet am ready to droop under a distrustful and unthankful dullness!'[64] Concerning hearing, he chimes, 'How sweetly doth this music sound in this dead season!'[65] The sense of touch: 'How benumbed and (for the time) senseless is this arm of mine become only with the too long leaning upon it!'[66] Smell: 'Methinks there is no earthly thing that yields so perfect a pleasure to any sense as the odor of the first rose doth to the scent.'[67] Finally, physical taste: 'How loathsome a draught is this, how offensive both to the eye and to the scent and to the taste!'[68] Throughout *Occasional Meditations* Hall models the skill, which was highly-valued in his day, of transforming every mundane object of perception into a conduit to God and Christ.

Having considered singing in this intellectual context, we learn several things. To a culture acutely aware of the material body, its pleasures, operations, and disabilities, singing became a central concern by virtue of its relationship with the sensual orbit. The voice requires no intermediary tools or instruments for its expression—a body is all that is needed. Singing is very much a visceral activity, for in vocalizing we experience physical sensations in the diaphragm, chest, throat, and head. One's entire body feels sympathetic resonance during singing. Baxter wrote concerning this kinesthetic sense that 'the delight of the sense of feeling ... is the greatest of all the rest.'[69] In the end, the ear and sense of hearing join the sensory cycle as performer and audience together hear the sound produced.

---

64 Joseph Hall, *Occasional Meditations* (1633), in Frank Livingstone Huntley, *Bishop Joseph Hall and Protestant Meditation in Seventeenth-Century England* (Binghamton, New York: Center for Medieval and Early Renaissance Studies, State University of New York at Binghamton, 1981), 130.

65 Ibid., 147.

66 Ibid., 157.

67 Ibid., 174.

68 Ibid., 196.

69 Baxter, *The Saints' Everlasting Rest,* 602.

The stature of vocal music in this culture as a sensual, yet innocent, delight was also enhanced by its participation within the three books of knowledge or sources of spiritual wisdom outlined above: the Book of Creatures, the Book of Conscience, and the Book of Scripture. Being a human skill, singing was considered a part of the first. Thomas Bradbury preached that it is 'different from Meditation, where the Soul is purely retired into itself, and shuts out the whole Creation'—rather, it is an outward manifestation of the inner processes of the soul, and has special value insofar as it publicly and sensibly engages the realm, or book, of creation. Devotional song's appeal to psychological intimacies (see chapter two) places it firmly within the Book of Conscience as well. Finally, its dependence upon the Book of Scripture is by now obvious.

In arguing that singing represents the safest and most wholesome expression of sensuality, Bradbury, like other English divines, bequeaths it with an archetypal, almost mythical status. Most fascinating is where he describes how singing plays a unique role in differentiating between proper and improper sensuality:

> Men will show their pleasure abroad. Such as are governed by a sensual Taste of things, feel a Delight that cannot be pent up. They declare themselves in Roaring and Folly, and an Excess of Riot. Now 'tis this Ordinance [singing] that fixes the distinction between profane and sacred Mirth.[70]

Singing signified so many things to early English Protestants. In chapter two we saw how closely it was linked to the application of the divine Word, personal comfort, and spiritual education. The voice, by virtue of its intermediary function as a symbolic neotype in the salvation drama, became a physical vehicle for expressing the most intimate and personal concerns of the soul. Chapter three traced the voice's effect upon the inward dynamics of the soul, the complex interplay between the will, rationality, and the affections. Now the body and the senses are incorporated into this vocal scheme as well. To refrain from singing the praises of God finally became viewed in this culture as a curiously bloodless aberration, a negation of the corporal self: 'Those Few Untuned Souls, who affect upon Principle to distinguish themselves from the rest of Mankind, by the Character of Non-Singers, do seem too much to divest themselves of an Humanity, whereof it may be said unto them, *Doth not nature it self teach it you?*'[71]

---

70 Thomas Bradbury, 'Arguments for the Duty of Singing' in *Practical Discourses of Singing*, 49.
71 Mather, *Accomplished Singer*, 1.

Chapter Five

Through the Gates of Paradise

Mercy: Hark; don't you hear a noise?

Christiana: Yes; 'tis, as I believe, a noise of music for joy that we are here.

Mercy: Wonderful! Music in the house, music in the heart, and music also in heaven, for joy that we are here.
—John Bunyan, *The Pilgrim's Progress*

With these words, Bunyan's allegorical characters neatly encapsulate the territory which singing occupied in the early English Protestant imagination. We know by now that singing of a most intimate nature did indeed occur within many English families during this era—'in the house'; and, following Christiana and Mercy's conversation further, we have traced ways in which singing was believed to shape the inward spiritual life, residing 'in the heart.' Finally, we concentrate on how singing represented the eschatological hope of the faith by symbolizing an unseen dimension existing within the present, as well as future ecstasies in heaven. When one took Wither's *Haleluiah* seriously as a guide, all of life was absorbed into song, for singing would provide comfort for all earthly ills, express all joys, and, in the end, complete the cycle as an emblem of eternal life.

Singing and the Christian Duties

With his comment, 'by singing we present unto our senses and minds the lively type of heavenly joys,' Nathanial Homes expresses his culture's belief that vocal music has the ability to transcend normal boundaries and communicate directly with the human psyche.[1] The era believed that the act of singing hymns and Psalms affected the human soul in a way that merely speaking them could not. How was this considered possible? William Ames, in his *Conscience with the Power and Cases Thereof*, specifically addresses the question 'what use hath singing above the ordinary pronunciation?' His answer:

---

1 Homes, *Gospel Musick*, 11.

1. It brings a kind of sweet delight to godly minds.
2. It hath a more distinct and fixed meditation.
3. It hath a more copious and ample profession of piety.
4. It hath more command of mutual edification, if it be with others.[2]

Points one, two and four have been previously covered, and we now focus on the idea that singing allows for a more abundant 'profession of piety.' While they would grant that sanctification can certainly take place without musical assistance, Anglican and Puritan divines held that singing somehow enhances and magnifies the experience of growth in Christian maturity: note the word 'more' in Ames's reply. They agreed that the soul who loves her Lord, proves this through song. Thomas Ford also contrasted singing to speech, and claimed that singing is a unique form of vocal expression because it represents the dichotomy of a temporal activity which fixes the mind upon eternal, timeless subject matter.

> There is more sweetness of meditation in singing, than in reading or the bare reciting of them. In singing there is a dilating of the sound, and a drawing out of the voice which gives us more time for the fixing of our hearts upon that which is sung, in a more sweet meditation of the goodness or power of God, or whatsoever the matter be ... The soul (I say) in singing is as it were, elevated and raised, and so comes to be more ravished with admiration of what God hath done.[3]

In calling singing a type of meditation, Ford exhibits the close relationship which developed in the English Protestant mind between singing and the Christian duties (or graces) of meditation, prayer, penitence, and praise. This underlines the high status of vocal music within early modern culture. Indeed, singing and meditation are so often mentioned within the same sentence that the two appear synonymous.

> If thou meditate seriously, God may enlighten thee in the very singing. We read and hear, to get more understanding, though sometimes we read and hear what for the present we understand not, and so ... we may sing also. Some, I am confident, have found by experience, that in singing of Psalms they have come to more understanding of some passages, than ever they had before.[4]

We also find singing identified with prayer. Singers are advised to 'fetch Lessons out of every Verse, and then turn them into Prayers, to form a Note

---

2 Ames, *Conscience*, 43.

3 Thomas Ford, *Singing of Psalmes the Duty of Christians Under the New Testament, or a Vindication of that Gospel-Ordinance in V. Sermons Upon Ephesians 5.19* (London, 1659), 72.

4 Ibid., 125.

and a Wish upon every clause before us.'[5] Like prayer, devotional singing was viewed as a form of communication with God, and shares with prayer an aura of sincerity and intimacy. Early modern divines discerned that prayer and song contain the same impulse of reaching out to something or someone else. The Anglican preacher Richard Allen noted that the Hebrew word for singing means to *extend*, and is related linguistically to the act of extending the eyes (to behold a thing diligently) and also to offering presents (where there is an 'extension of the hand').[6] Psalms and hymns became valued as a type of metaphorical incense: 'No doubt but the songs of the faithful may be as a sweet odor of incense unto him.'[7] Homes summarized that 'singing is nothing else but a more deliberate, distinct, pausing, and mediating praying.'

Singing was connected to the dark hues of penitence as well. The late medieval church had strained the dynamic of penitence/salvation to a breaking point with its endowed masses and sales of indulgences. The Protestant Reformation swept all this away at the same time that it re-emphasized the yawning chasm between God and man. So, although the Reformers rejected any idea of an intrinsically meritorious worth to penance, raising the soul to the appropriate level of grief remained an important concern among Anglicans and Puritans, who agreed that 'the way to prevent everlasting trouble, is to desire to be troubled with a preventing trouble.'[8] Singing was the perfect agent to spur on such a spiritual crisis:

> It is most certain also, upon exceeding good experience, that singing of Psalms hath mightily humbled the soul even to tears. The Psalm after a Sermon sometimes hath done that which the Sermon alone could not do. The Sermon as it were turned the wind into a warm quarter to begin to thaw the soul: and then the Psalm hath been as the breaking out of the Sun-beams, to make the heart run with melting.[9]

But even the most doctrinaire minds recognized that life does not consist entirely of sighing over sin; thus, we find singing most often linked with the supreme function in this scheme—praise. Incorporating praise into daily life through song was believed to perform a kind of regulatory function over the homeostasis of the soul, as seen in chapter three. The ultimate end of praise was a type of absorption into the transcendent: 'the Faith and Hope, that are contending upwards, do never so well employ themselves, as in the Duty of admiring God; because it's so much the same with the vision

---

5 Mather, *Accomplished Singer*, 14.
6 Singing is primarily 'an extension of the voice,' Richard Allen, *An Essay to prove Singing of Psalms with conjoin'd Voices, a Christian Duty: And to resolve the Doubts concerning it* (London 1696), 29.
7 *The Praise of Musicke*, 147.
8 Sibbes, *Soules Conflict*, 88.
9 Homes, *Gospel Musick*, 9.

into which they shall expire.'[10] Choir singers correspondingly took on a mediatory role in worship: 'In a sense he is making of you, his spiritual priests, to offer up, in his Church the spiritual Sacrifices of praise unto Him!'[11] Such sentiments confirmed vocal music's reputation as a balm and medicine for the spirit. According to John Newte, singing could even provide a (partial) remedy for the Fall's corruption. 'Artificial songs ... supply the Defects and ... assist in Repairing that voice of Joy and gladness in serving the Lord, which had been miserably broken by Disobedience and Sin.'[12] In a very real sense, then, singing the praises of God was believed to bring heaven down to earth: 'perhaps we can form no truer Conception of the Work of Heaven than this.'[13]

'An Entrance into Glory'

Unfortunately, the cliché of greeting-card angels lolling about on marshmallowy clouds and playing harps has perhaps blinded us to a significant aspect of Reformed doctrine—its eschatology. Following the path of scripture and early church theologians, English divines wrote profusely on the place of singing in heaven. In their book *Heaven: A History*, Colleen McDannell and Bernhard Lang trace various western Christian interpretations of eternity over two millenia. In their view, the Reformation, in contrast to the contemplative, intellectual vision of Aquinas, and the humanist Renaissance ideal of the paradise garden, promoted the concept of a theocentric heaven.[14] One question which has consistantly baffled theologians is, what does one *do* in heaven? It is hard for us, after all, to envision perfection. Will the souls and glorified bodies be active or passive? Within the theocentric model, saints and angels together will be singing the praises of God in *active* worship (this differs from the medieval view, which assigned the bulk of singing duty to angels). According to McDannell and Lang, Richard Baxter is to be credited with rediscovering the 'Augustinian emphasis on everlasting praise'; but this theme (with its vocal ramifications) actually pervades seventeenth-century Anglican and Puritan literature.[15] Again we see the typical English

---

10 Bradbury, 'Arguments for the Duty of Singing' in *Practical Discourses of Singing,* 54.

11 Hedge, *Duty and Manner,* 38.

12 John Newte, *The Lawfulness and Use of Organs in the Christian Church, Asserted in a Sermon preach'd at Tiverton in the county of Devon upon the 13th of September,* 1696 (London, 1696), 6.

13 Harris, 'The Excellence of the Duty of Singing' in *Practical Discourses of Singing,* 88.

14 McDannell and Lang consider this a characteristic of western Christianity in general during the seventeenth century.

15 Colleen McDannell and Bernhard Lang, *Heaven: A History* (Yale University Press, 1988), 173.

Protestant call for an individual response within piety. Yet singers in the afterlife will not be singing alone; they will join the throng worshipping the Lamb. Heaven will be a community, the largest community ever imagined. Some writers hint that the barrier between earth and eternity can even be broached: Thomas Ravenscroft notes that Christian singers mystically participate with 'the choir of Angels and Saints,' whose perpetual duty in heaven 'is to sing their concording parts without pause.'[16] Mather claims that

> the Angels take a more singular and special Delight in doing of Good Offices for those who by Spiritual Songs are more associated with them; always on the Wing to be their Guardians. And Oh! how much of Heaven have hundreds of thousands found coming down into their souls, while they have attempted thus to come into a Consort with the angels there! ... It is beyond what any Tongue may utter, or any heart conceive.[17]

Singing is used as an ultimate symbol of earthly happiness as well. In general, we have problems with superlatives in old books. We tend to dismiss them as either rhetorical blustering or an author's toadying up to some wealthy patron—in neither case are the words taken very seriously. Yet they reveal a lot about a writer's or society's order of value; and the fact that these divines reserved their highest praise for singing confirms its weight within this culture. Baxter, for instance, promises that 'one strain of ... celestial melody, doth afford more ravishing sweetness and delight, than all that ever earth could yield.'[18] Note his use of superlatives in this passage from *The Saints' Everlasting Rest:*

> Singing of praise is a most profitable duty, because it is so delightful, as it were, to God himself, that he hath made it his people's eternal work; for they shall sing the song of Moses, and the song of the Lamb. As desire, and faith, and hope, are of shorter continuance than love and joy, so also preaching, and prayer, and sacraments, and all means for confirmation, and expression of faith and hope, shall cease, when our thanks, and praise, and triumphant expressions of love and joy, shall abide for ever. The liveliest emblem of heaven that I know upon earth, is, when the people of God ... do join together ... in the cheerful and melodious singing of his praises.[19]

The literature is replete with similar testimonials. Ford echoes Baxter: 'I believe that godly men ... have scarcely seen more of God in any Exercise than in this. To my thinking, there is not a more lively resemblance of

---

16 Thomas Ravenscroft, *The Whole Booke of Psalms: with the Hymnes Evangelicall, and Songs Spirituall* (London, 1621), preface.
17 Mather, *Accomplished Singer*, 10.
18 Baxter, *Right Rejoycing*, 21.
19 Baxter, *The Saints' Everlasting Rest*, 543.

heaven upon earth, than a company of godly Christians singing a Psalm together.'[20] On the royalist Anglican side, Lord Coleraine concludes that 'these Spiritual Songs ... contain not only the Body and Substance, but the Spirit and Quintessence, the pleasant Tastes, the best Relishes of our holiest Religion!'[21] Another indicator of singing's value within this society was the way it was used to culminate ecstatic passages. Rous rhapsodizes in *The Arte of Happiness*:

> In the infinite love of God, [the love of the glorified Soul] still steepeth and drowneth it self; and the more it seeth the Love of God, the more it loves God; and the more it loves God, the more it is beloved. And out of the feeling of this surpassing Love of God, break out those Songs of Joy, and Voices of Exultation.[22]

Singing captured the crown of earthly delights within the English Protestant imagination. It was credited with more mystical characteristics as well. In a fantastic passage from *The Accomplished Singer*, Mather claims that singing helps the believer intuit invisible spiritual realities existing in the future:

> The Devout Singer like the Beloved disciple [John, author of Revelation] shall be carried away in the Spirit into the Wilderness, and be shown the Judgment of the Great Whore, that sitteth upon many Waters. He shall also in these Visions of God, see the Holy City, New Jerusalem, coming down from God out of Heaven, prepared as a Bride for her Husband. Very depraved must be that Soul, that has not a relish for such Contemplations, more than for any Earthly Entertainments; and that will not heartily say, They're more desirable than Gold, yea, than much solid Gold; than Honey also sweeter much, or dropping Honey-Comb.[23]

Like the *logos*, singing represents an eternal constant. From word to song, this study ends by closing the circle. Early English Protestants were convinced that, as saints, they would someday experience the full pleasure of singing which was as yet unknown to them. In the meanwhile, singing connected them to an unseen current which existed from the dawn of time when the world was first vocalized into being. As one clergyman put it, 'As the apostle prefers Charity, before all other Christian graces, because it never faileth; so may we prefer singing before all other Christian duties,

---

20 Ford, *Singing of Psalmes*, 99.
21 Lord Coleraine [Henry Hare], *The Ascent of the Soul: or, David's Mount towards God's House. Being Paraphrases on the fifteen Psalms of Degrees* (London, 1665), n.p.
22 Francis Rous, *The Arte of Happiness* (London, 1619), 502.
23 Mather, *Accomplished Singer*, 20.

because it will never be laid aside—a whole eternity will be employed in singing anthems of praise to God and to the Lamb.'[24]

Conclusion

Having entered the world of early modern Anglican and Puritan divines, it is clear why singing captured their fascination so completely. For singing represented a universal activity which could, Janus-like, show different faces as circumstances warranted. It signified good times and companionship, the comforts of home and hearth, a lifeline for the sick and dying, and boys with fresh-scrubbed faces piping in the divine service—but it carried other deeper meanings as well, which appealed to the heightened spiritual sensibilities of the day. These devotional writers believed that singing had the power to reconcile the basic dichotomies of human existence of holiness versus pleasure, spirit versus body, and reason versus imagination. In short, singing drew them because within this simple act they discerned *wholeness:* a smooth cooperation of physical and mental forces, capable of creating (almost incidentally) great beauty.

Since the theologians cited throughout this book operated within a Protestant Christian framework, much of what they wrote concerning the transformational power of singing depended, in their opinion, upon an individual having been converted, thus possessing the necessary quality of a 'tender,' or regenerate, heart. Baxter, Hall, and the rest would have been the last to imply that devotional singing benefits the atheist or pagan in equal measure as the believer—for how, they would argue, could a creature who neglects its Creator be properly grateful for (or even fully aware of) his gifts? At the same time, everyone agreed that singing was a pleasant gift from God, a phenomenon of common grace which, like the rain, 'falls on the just and unjust alike.' They recognized that to sing was an impulse shared by all. John Cotton observed, for example, that 'singing with heart and voice is a moral worship, such as is written in the hearts of all men by nature.'[25] So singing could exert its grace, albeit to a lesser extent, upon all types of people. Explaining why even non-believers are indebted to sing to God's glory, Thomas Bradbury remarked:

> Though the Mysteries of Redemption are unknown among them, so that they cannot think of God's loving kindness in the midst of his Temple; yet Creation and Providence give them the Memorials of a Deity, and those may touch their Joys in a fainter way.[26]

---

24 Hedge, *Duty and Manner*, 17.
25 Cotton, *Singing of the Psalms*, 5.
26 Bradbury, 'Arguments for the Duty of Singing,' in *Practical Discourses of Singing*, 23.

Following along these somewhat more ecumenical lines, I do think it is possible to extrapolate from these sources certain universal qualities about this 'memorial of a deity' without doing too much violence to their original intentions or casting any aspersions upon their theology. If we take a step back and ask the famous question, 'what does it *mean*?' several themes from the literature immediately spring to mind.

First of all, throughout these writings singing signifies an aesthetic of *inner sincerity and integrity*, a unity of heart and voice joined with a certain gravity and reliability of expression. The dictionary defines sincerity as 'freedom from fraud and deceit,' and we have seen a repeated emphasis upon the importance of appraising oneself honestly, and then relaying that essence forthrightly in all communications, musical and otherwise. In this way, the singer becomes an oracle who summons the proper affections from deep inside to match the outward, textual meaning of lyrics—and in the course of doing so, communicates something of his inner personality which may or may not be readily apparent offstage.

I propose that it is this very capacity of singing, to reveal intimate qualities about the self, which accounts for the extraordinary reticence most modern people feel about singing in public. Voice teachers know that teaching our craft is quite different from giving lessons on an instrument such as cello or piano, for the simple reason that we encounter so much reluctance, and sometimes sheer terror, from beginners at the prospect of vocalizing in front of another soul. A good voice teacher has to be somewhat of an amateur psychologist. It is common for students to panic, cry, hyperventilate, even feel physically ill while singing. If we take a moment to ask ourselves why this should be so—after all, no gets upset when asked to plunk a note on the piano or blow into a clarinet—it seems that the implicit nakedness of the singing act has a great deal to do with this universal shyness.

Secondly, singing connotes *emotional passion*, the capacity to experience profound feelings and empathize with others more fully. This finds a twentieth-century parallel in *How the Grinch Stole Christmas!* The Grinch hates Christmas and everything associated with it because his heart is 'two sizes too small.' Even the big blue eyes of little Cindy Lou when she spies him stealing her Christmas tree do not move him. What causes his conversion at the end of the story? It is the sound of Who-ville singing, greeting Christmas morning which makes the Grinch's heart grow 'three times'—and, like Scrooge, he becomes a generous and empathetic soul. Singing 'overturns' the Grinch's heart like nothing else can. Chapter three traced the early modern ideal of the soul: a serene and orderly confidence, characterized by joy, discouraged by outward circumstances only momentarily, and punctuated by that highest strain of all the affections, holy zeal. English Protestants over three hundred years ago would have agreed with the Romantic sentiment that to live without feeling is to scarcely live at all.[27]

Singing also signifies *intellectual engagement and organization*. This concept challenges modern assumptions about the artistic process and temperament. Fond of dividing the mind's functions into left and right brain, we prefer to think of singing as an imaginative, non-rational activity over a highly rational one. The early modern era, however, did not posit such extremes, for it viewed the mind as a complex blend of imagination, affections, and will, all submissive in the end to reason. Because of this, education was always high on their lists of rationales for singing, and the psalters and hymnals which became a musical catechism for English and colonial populations bore out this philosophy. In our own day, recent cognitive studies seem to affirm a link between music and intellectual performance. Perhaps directed singing can even help stave off mental decline in older populations? The possibility is intriguing.

Singing also references an aesthetic of *meaningful privacy and solitude*. It is unusual and a bit intriguing to see the subject of what one does when alone addressed so forthrightly. We have seen how the practice of private devotional singing shared with the prayer closet the intangible aims of personal solace and moral improvement, and how both were foundational to the era's concept of spirituality

At the same time, it signifies *family and community unity*. Anglican and Puritan divines believed that the act of raising voices together was one of the best ways to build relationships and strengthen already-existing ties. I think again of John Coad's account of men trapped in the claustrophic confines of a prison ship who, scourged by lice and dysentary, found the strength to croak out psalm tunes they had probably learned in childhood. In such a bare struggle for existence as this, who is to say that the mutual encouragement thus gained may not be the deciding factor between life and death?

Finally, singing connotes *transcendent striving*. As prayer represents a mental reaching out with one's thoughts and hopes, so singing connotes a similar reaching out with the physical voice. Early English Protestants, like modern Christians, directed their hymns to the biblical God, the Father, Son, and Holy Ghost, but the idea of singing to an unseen force is not restricted to them. Most cultures articulate a related idea that singing (in its highest form) symbolizes a musical offering and sacrifice—to a deity, or, if one prefers, to a non-sectarian 'spirit' of music.

In closing, if any of my readers remain unconvinced, I ask them to take these directions for worshippers from an early eighteenth-century Presbyterian minister and compare them to the stage behavior we have come to expect from song recitalists today:

---

27 Dr. Seuss, *How the Grinch Stole Christmas!* (New York: Random House, 1957).

In this Duty the Head must be uncovered, the Countenance composed and serious, the Eye fixed, not roving and wandering; and, in a word, the whole external Behaviour such, as in the judgment of Charity, bespeaks an engaged and devout Mind and Heart, and as becomes the Perfections of the God we worship. And whether that Posture in Singing, which generally obtains among us, be so proper for psalms of direct Prayer and Praise, I leave to your own serious deliberate Considerations.[28]

Throughout these chapters we have seen how the act of singing became conflated to take on extra-musical functions in English society. Singing represented the happy marriage of the rational and emotive sides of the soul. It was also the means by which common believers could identify with heroic characters and gain personal solace. An archaic song genre thus offers some surprising insights on performance, aesthetic motivations, and even basic questions of sensuality versus rationality. In the end, we realize that a different era knew more complex and intriguing musical motivations than we might ever have expected.

---

28 Newman, 'Directions for the right Performance of the Duty of Singing,' in *Practical Discourses of Singing,* 166

Bibliography

Primary Sources

Adams, Thomas. *The Sacrifice of Thankefulnesse*. London, 1616.

Allen, Richard. *An Essay to prove Singing of Psalms with conjoin'd Voices, a Christian Duty: And to resolve the Doubts concerning it*. London, 1696.

Ames, William. *Conscience with the power and causes thereof [De conscientia], in five books*. London, 1639.

Andrewes, Lancelot. *The Private Devotions of the right Reverend Father in God Lancelot Andrewes*. London, 1647.

Augustine of Hippo. *Confessions*. Vernon J. Bourke (tr.) New York: Fathers of the Church, Inc. 1953.

B. A. Philo-Mus. *Synopsis of Vocal Musick: Containing the Rudiments of Singing Rightly any Harmonical Song, delivered In a Method so Solid, Short and Plain, that this Art may now be Learned more exactly, speedily and Easily, than ever heretofore. Whereunto are added Several Psalms and Songs of Three Parts. Composed by English and Italian Authors for the benefits of young Beginners*. London, 1680.

Bathe, William. *A Briefe Introduction to the skill of Song*. London, 1596.

Baxter, Richard. *A Christian Directory*. London, 1673.

_____ *The Divine Life*. London, 1664.

_____ *Poetical Fragments: Heart-Imployment with God and It Self*. London, 1681.

_____ *The Reasons of the Christian Religion, The First Part, Of Godliness: Proving by Natural Evidence the Being of God: the Necessity of Holiness, and a future Life of Retribution. the Sinfulness of the World; the Desert of Hell; and what hope of Recovery Mercies intimate. The Second Part, Of Christianity: Proving by Evidence Supernatural and Natural, the certain Truth of the Christian Belief: First meditated for the well-settling of his own Belief; and now published for the benefit of others*. London, 1667.

_____ *Right Rejoycing: or, The Nature and Order of Rational and Warrantable Joy*. London, 1660.

_____ *The Saints' Everlasting Rest, or, A treatise of the blessed state of the saints in their enjoyment of God in glory*. London, 1651. London: William Tegg and Co., 1854.

Bayly, Lewis. *The Practice of Pietie: Directing a Christian how to walk that he may please God*. London, 1612.

Bedford, Arthur. *The Great Abuse of Music*. London, 1711.

_____ *The Temple Musick*. London, 1706.

Bernard of Clairvaux. *A Rule of Good Life*. London, 1633; reprint, *English Recusant Literature* 1558-1640 series, D.M. Rogers (ed.), no. 79. Yorkshire: Scolar Press, 1971.

Bernard, Richard. *Iosuah's Godly Resolution in conference with Caleb, touching household governement for well-ordering a familie*. London, 1612.

Bolton, Robert. *Mr. Bolton's Foure Last Things: Death, Judgement, Hell, Heaven*. London, 1631.

_____ *The Saints Sure and Perpetuall Guide or, A Treatise concerning the Word*. London, 1634.

_____ *Some Generall Directions for a Comfortable Walking with God*. 1625.

Brady, Nicholas. *Church Musick Vindicated*. London, 1697.

Brathwayt, Richard. *Essays Upon the Five Senses*. London, 1625.

Brookbank, Joseph. *The Well-tuned Organ, or, an Exercitation: wherein, This Question is fully and largely discussed, Whether or no Instrumental, and Organical Musick be lawful in Holy Publick Assemblies?* London, 1660.

Bunyan, John. *The Pilgrim's Progress from this world to that which is to come*. London, 1678.

Burney, Charles. *A General History of Music from the Earliest Ages to the Present Period*. London, 1782-9.

Butler, Charles. *The Principles of Musik, in Singing and Setting: with the two-fold Use thereof, (Ecclesiasticall and Civil)*. London, 1636.

Byfield, Nicholas. *An Exposition Upon the Epistle to the Colossians*. London, 1617.

Caccini, Giulio. *Le Nuove Musiche*. H. Wiley Hitchcock (ed.) Madison, WI: A-R Editions, Inc., 1970.

Calamy, Edmund. *The Art of Divine Meditation*. London, 1680.

Calvin, Jean. *Institutes of the Christian Religion*. Henry Beveridge (tr.) Grand Rapids, MI: Wm. B. Eerdmans Publishing Co., 1962.

Coad, John. *A Memorandum of the Wonderful Providences of God to a poor unworthy Creature, during the time of the Duke of Monmouth's Rebellion and to the Revolution in 1688*. London: Longman, Brown, Green, & Longmans, 1849.

Coleraine, Lord. (Henry Hare). *The Ascent of the Soul: or, David's Mount towards God's House*. London, 1665.

_____ La Scala Santa: or, *A Scale of Devotions Musical and Gradual: being Descants on the fifteen Psalms of Degrees, in metre; with Contemplations and Collects upon them, in prose*. London, 1670.

Cotton, John. *Singing of the Psalms a Gospel-Ordinance*. London, 1647.

Dennis, John. *Essay on the Operas after the Italian Manner, which are about to be established on the English Stage: With some Reflections on the Damage which they may bring the Publick*. London, 1706.

Dingley, Robert. *The Spirituall Taste Described*. London, 1649.

Dodwell, Henry. *A Treatise concerning the Lawfulness of Instrumental Musick in Holy Offices*. London, 1700.

Donne, John. *Sermons*. George R. Potter and Evelyn M. Simpson (eds.) Berkeley: University of California Press, 1959.

Dr. Seuss. *How the Grinch Stole Christmas!* New York: Random House, 1957.

Evelyn, John. *Diaries*. E.S. de Beer (ed.) London: Oxford University Press, 1959.

Featley, Daniel. *Ancilla Pietatis: or, the Hand-Maid to private Devotion: presenting a Manuall to her Mistresse, furnished with Instructions, Hymnes and Prayers.* London, 1647.

Fenner, William. *A Treatise of the Affections.* London, 1641.

_____ *The Efficacie of Importunate Prayer.* London, 1657.

_____ *The Use and Benefit of Divine Meditation.* London, 1657.

Ford, Thomas. *Singing of Psalmes the Duty of Christians Under the New Testament, or a Vindication of that Gospel-Ordinance in V. Sermons Upon Ephesians 5.19.* London, 1659.

H., E. *Scripture Proof for Singing of Scripture Psalms, Hymns and Spiritual Songs: or, An Answer to several Queries and Objections frequently made use of to stumble and turn aside young Christians from their Duty to God in Singing of Psalms.* London, 1696.

Hall, John. *The Court of Vertue.* London, 1565.

Hall, Joseph. *Christ Mysticall: or, The blessed union of Christ and his Members.* London, 1647.

_____ *The Devout Soul, or Rules of heavenly devotion.* London, 1644.

_____ *An Holy Rapture: or, A Patheticall Mediation of the love of Christ.* London, 1647.

_____ *Select Thoughts, One Century, also the Breathings of the Devout Soul.* London, 1648.

Hedge, Lemuel. *The duty and manner of singing in Christian churches.* Boston, 1772.

Holder, William. *A Treatise of the Natural Grounds, and Principles of Harmony.* London, 1694.

Homes, Nathaniel. *Gospel Musick. Or, the Singing of Davids Psalms, &c. In the public Congregations, or private Families asserted, and vindicated.* London, 1644.

Hooker, Richard. *Of the Laws of Ecclesiastical Polity, in The Works of that Learned and judicious divine Mr. Richard Hooker, with an account of his life and death by Isaac Walton.* John Keble, R.W. Church, and F. Paget (eds.) Oxford: Clarendon Press, 1888.

Ignatius of Loyola. *Spiritual Exercises.* W.H. Longridge (tr.) London: Robert Scott Roxburghe House, 1919.

Ingelo, Nathaniel. *Bentivolio and Urania.* London, 1660.

Julian of Norwich. *Juliana, anchoret, 1343-1443: A Book of Showings to the Anchoress Julian of Norwich.* Edmund Colledge and James Walsh (eds.) Toronto: Pontifical Institute of Mediaeval Studies, 1978.

Keach, Benjamin. *The Breach Repaired in God's Worship: or, singing of Psalms, Hymns, and Spiritual Songs, proved to be an holy Ordinance of Jesus Christ.* London, 1691.

Mace, Thomas. *Musick's Monument: or, a Rembrancer Of the Best Practical Musick, Both Divine, and Civil, that has ever been known, to have been in the World.* London, 1676.

Mason, John. *Spiritual Songs*. London, 1696.

Mather, Cotton. *The Accomplished Singer. Instructions How the Piety of Singing with a True Devotion, may be obtained and expressed; the Glorious God after an uncommon manner Glorified in it, and His people Edified*. Boston, 1721.

Morley, Thomas. *A Plaine and Easie Introduction to Practicall Musicke*. London, 1597.

Newte, John. *The Lawfulnesse and Use of Organs in the Christian Church. Asserted in a Sermon preach'd at Tiverton in the county of Devon upon the 13th of September, 1696*. London, 1696.

North, Roger. *The Musicall Grammarian*. London, 1728.

Ornithoparcus, Andreas. *Andreas Ornithoparcus His Micrologus, or Introduction: Containing the Art of Singing*. John Dowland (tr.) London, 1609.

Owen, John. *A Discourse of the Work of the Holy Spirit in Prayer. With a brief Enquiry into the Nature and Use of Mental Prayer and Forms*. London, 1682.

_____ *The Grace and Duty of Being Spiritually-Minded*. London, 1681.

_____ *Of Communion with God the Father, Sonne, and Holy Ghost, each Person Distinctly: in Love, Grace, and Consolation: or, The Saints Fellowship with the Father, Sonne, and Holy Ghost, Unfolded*. Oxford, 1657.

Peacham, Henry. *The Complete Gentleman*. London, 1622.

Perkins, William. *A Cloud of Faithfull Witnesses, Leading To The Heavenly Canaan: Or, A Commentarie upon the eleventh Chapter to the Hebrewes*. London, 1622.

_____ *The Whole Treatise of The Cases of Conscience*. London, 1631.

Playford, John. *A Breefe Introduction to the Skill of Music for Song and Violl*. London, 1654.

Practical Discourses of Singing in the Worship of God, By Several Ministers. London, 1708.

The Praise of Musicke. London, 1586.

Prelleur, Peter. *The Modern Musick-Master, or, the Universal Musician*. London, 1731.

Preston, John. *The Breast Plate of Faith and Love*. London, 1630.

_____ *The Fulnesse of Christ for Us: A Sermon preached at the Court before King James of Blessed Memory*. London, 1640.

_____ *The Saints' Daily Exercise: A Treatise Unfolding the Whole Dutie of Prayer*. London, 1629.

Ravenscroft, Thomas. *The Whole Booke of Psalmes: with the Hymnes Evangelicall, and Songs Spirituall*. London, 1621.

Reynoldes, Edward. *A Treatise of the Passions and Faculties of the Soul of Man*. London, 1647.

Rimbault, Edward F. (ed.) *The Old Cheque-book, or, Book of Remembrance of the Chapel Royal from 1561-1744*. New York: Da Capo Press, 1966.

Rous, Francis. *The Arte of Happiness*. London, 1619.

_____ *The Heavenly Academie: or the highest school, Where alone is that highest Teaching, the Teaching of the Heart*. London, 1638.

_____ *The Mysticall Marriage, or, Experimentall Discoveries of the heavenly Marriage betweene a Soule and her Saviour*. London, 1635.

Sibbes, Richard. *Divine Meditations and Holy Contemplations*. London, 1638.

_____ *A Glance of Heaven. Or, a Pretious Taste of a glorious Feast. Wherein thou mayst taste and see those things which God hath prepared for them that love him.* London, 1638.

_____ *Light from Heaven in foure Treatises.* London, 1638.

_____ *The Saints' Cordialls.* London, 1637.

_____ *The Soules Conflict with it Selfe: and victory over it selfe by Faith.* London, 1635.

Simpson, Christopher. *A Compendium of Practical Musick.* London, 1667.

Sparke, Michael. *The Crums of Comfort, with Godly Prayers.* London, 1623.

Strunk, Oliver (ed.) *Source Readings in Music History: From Classical Antiquity through the Romantic Era.* New York: W.W. Norton & Company, 1950.

Sydenham, Hymphrey. *The Well-Tuned Cymball, Or, a Vindication of the Moderne Harmony and Ornaments in our Churches. Against the Murmuring of their discontented Opposers.* London, 1637.

Symson, Andrew. *Spiritual Songs, or Holy Poems. A Garden of true Delight, All the Scripture-songs that are not in the Book of Psalms, together with several sweet Prophetical and Evangelical Scriptures, meet to be composed into Songs, Translated into English Meeter, and fitted to be sung with any of the common Tunes of the Psalms.* Edinburgh, 1685.

Tosi, Pietro. *Observations on the Florid Song: or Sentiments on the Ancient and Modern Singer. Translated by J.E. Galliard.* London, 1742.

Ussher, James. *A Method for Meditation: or, A Manuall of Divine Duties.* London, 1657.

Watts, Isaac. *The Beauties of the late Reverend Dr. Isaac Watts.* London, 1782.

_____ *Divine Songs, Attempted in Easy Language for the use of Children.* London, 1715.

_____ *The World to Come: or Discourses on the Joys or Sorrows of Departed Souls at Death, and the Glory or Terror of the Resurrection.* London, 1738.

Wither, George. *Haleluiah, or Britan's Second Remembrancer, bringing to Remembrance (in praisefull and Penitentiall Hymns, Spirituall Songs, and Morall-Odes) Meditations, advancing the glory of God in the practise of Pietie and Vertue; and applyed to easie Tunes, to be Sung in Families, &c.* London, 1641; reprint, Manchester: Spenser Society, Charles E. Simms, 1879.

_____ *The Hymnes and Songs of the Church.* London, 1623.

_____ *A Preparation to the Psalter.* London, 1619.

Wright, Thomas. *The Passions of the Mind in Generall.* London, 1604.

Secondary Sources

Studies in Music and Musical Thought

Anderson, Ronald. 'Richard Alison's Psalter (1599) and Devotional Music in England to 1640.' Ph.D. diss., University of Iowa, 1974.

Brown, Susan Tara. 'English Devotional Song as a Mirror of Seventeenth- Century Anglicanism: A Thematic and Musical-Rhetorical Analysis of Henry Playford's *Harmonia Sacra.*' Ph.D. diss., Claremont Graduate University, 1995.

Buelow, George J. 'Music, Rhetoric, and the Concept of the Affections: A Selective Bibliography.' *Notes of the Music Library Association* 30 (September 1973): 250-259.

Burnett, Charles, Michael Fend, and Penelope Gouk (eds.) *The Second Sense: Studies in Hearing and Musical Judgement from Antiquity to the Seventeenth Century.* London: The Warburg Institute, University of London, 1991.

Butler, Gregory G. 'Music and Rhetoric in Early Seventeenth-Century English Sources.' *Music Quarterly* 66 (January 1980): 53-64.

Caldwell, John, Edward Olleson, and Susan Wollenberg (eds.) *The Well Enchanting Skill: Music, Poetry, and Drama in the Culture of the Renaissance.* Oxford: Clarendon Press, 1990.

Dearnley, Christopher. *English Church Music in Royal Chapel, Cathedral and Parish Church 1650-1750.* London: Barrie and Jenkins, 1970.

Doughtie, Edward. *English Renaissance Song.* Boston: Twayne Publishers, 1986.

Eggleston, Rosalie J. 'A Study of Some Relationships between Late Renaissance Music and "The Temple" of George Herbert.' Ph.D. diss., University of New Mexico, 1969.

Escott, Harry. *Isaac Watts, Hymnographer: A Study of the Beginnings, Development, and Philosophy of the English Hymn.* London: Independent Press Ltd., 1962.

Faulkner, Quentin. *Wiser than Despair: The Evolution of Ideas in the Relationship of Music and the Christian Church.* Westport, Connecticut: Greenwood Press, 1996.

Finney, Gretchen L. 'Ecstasy and Music in Seventeenth-Century England.' *Journal of the History of Ideas* 8 (April 1947): 153-186.

_____ *Musical Backgrounds for English Literature: 1580-1650.* New Brunswick: Rutgers University Press, n.d.

_____ ' "Organical Musick" and Ecstasy.' *Journal of the History of Ideas* 8 (June 1947): 273-292.

Glass, Henry Alexander. *The Story of the Psalters: A History of the Metrical Versions of Great Britain and America.* London: Kegan Paul, Trench & Co., 1888.

Gouk, Penelope. *Music, Science, and Natural Magic in Seventeenth-Century England.* New Haven: Yale University Press, 1999.

Harran, Don. 'Directions to Singers in Writings of the Early Renaissance.' *Revue belge de musicologie* 41 (1987): 45-61.

_____ *Word-Tone Relations in Musical Thought: From Antiquity to the Seventeenth Century.* Stuttgart: American Institute of Musicology, Hanssler-Verlag, 1986.

Harley, John. *Music in Purcell's London: The Social Background.* London: Dennis Dobson, 1968.

Hollander, John. *The Untuning of the Sky: Ideas of Music in English Poetry 1500-1700.* Princeton: Princeton University Press, 1961.

Jensen, H. James. 'English Restoration Attitudes Towards Music.' *Musical Quarterly* 55 (1969): 206-214.

Jorgens, Elise Bickford. *The Well-Tun'd Word: Musical Interpretations of English Poetry 1597-1651.* Minneapolis: University of Minnesota Press, 1982.

Kime, Mary W. 'Lyric and Song: Seventeenth-Century Musical Settings of John Donne's Poetry.' Ph.D. diss., University of Denver, 1969.

Landon, Esther Abrams. 'Seventeenth and Eighteenth Century English and Colonial American Music Texts: An Analysis of Instructional Content.' Ph.D. diss., University of California Los Angeles, 1977.

Le Huray, Peter. *Music and the Reformation in England 1549-1660*. New York: Oxford University Press, 1967.

Mellers, Wilfrid. *Harmonious Meeting: a Study of the Relationship between English Music, Poetry and Theatre, c. 1600-1900*. London: Dennis Dobson, 1965.

Morehen, John (ed.). *English Choral Practice 1400-1650*. Cambridge: Cambridge University Press, 1995.

Munstedt, Peter Alan. 'John Playford, Music Publisher: A Bibliographical Catalogue.' Ph.D. diss., University of Kentucky, 1983.

Nelson, Russell Clair. 'John Playford and the English Amateur Musician.' Ph.D. diss., University of Iowa, 1966.

Potter, John. *Vocal Authority: Singing Style and Ideology*. Cambridge: Cambridge University Press, 1998.

Rainbow, Bernarr. *The Land without Music: Musical Education in England 1800-1860 and its continental antecedents*. London: Novello and Co. Ltd, 1967.

Sadie, Stanley (ed.). *The New Grove Dictionary of Music and Musicians*. London: Macmillan, 1980.

_____ *The New Grove Dictionary of Opera*. London: Macmillan, 1992.

Schleiner, Louise. 'Herbert's Divine and Moral Songs: Song-text Features in "The Temple" and their importance for Herbert's Poetic Idiom.' Ph.D. diss., Brown University, 1973.

_____ 'The Composer as Reader: a Setting of George Herbert's Altar.' *Musical Quarterly* 61 (1975): 422-432.

_____ *The Living Lyre in English Verse from Elizabeth through the Restoration*. Columbia: University of Missouri Press, 1984.

Scholes, Percy. *The Puritans and Music in England and New England: A Contribution to the Cultural History of Two Nations*. London: Oxford University Press, 1934.

Shapiro, Alexander. 'Drama of an Infinitely Superior Nature: Handel's Early English Oratorios and the Religious Sublime.' *Music and Letters* 74 (May 1993): 215-245.

Smallman, Basil. 'Endor Revisited: English Biblical Dialogues of the Seventeenth Century.' *Music and Letters* 46 (1965): 137-145.

Smith, Hallett. 'English Metrical Psalms in the Sixteenth Century and their Literary Significance.' *Huntington Library Quarterly* 9 (February 1946): 249-271.

Smith, Ruth. *Handel's Oratorios and Eighteenth-Century Thought*. Cambridge: Cambridge University Press, 1995.

Spinks, Ian. 'English Seventeenth-Century Dialogues.' *Music and Letters* 37 (1957): 155-163.

_____ *English Song: Dowland to Purcell*. New York: Scribner, 1974.

Temperly, Nicholas. *The Music of the English Parish Church*. Cambridge: Cambridge University Press, 1979.

Toft, Robert. *Tune Thy Musicke To Thy Hart: The Art of Eloquent Singing in England 1597-1622*. Toronto: University of Toronto Press, 1993.

Treacy, Susan. 'English Devotional Song of the Seventeenth-Century in Printed Collections from 1638 to 1693: A Study of Music and Culture.' Ph.D. diss., North Texas State University, 1986.

Westrup, J.A. 'Domestic Music Under the Stuarts.' *Royal Musical Association Proceedings* (March 1942): 19-53.

_____ 'The Chapel Royal Under James II.' *The Monthly Musical Record* (December 1940): 219-222.

Wilson, Ruth M. *Anglican Chant and Chanting in England, Scotland, and America 1660 to 1820.* Oxford: Clarendon Press, 1996.

Zimmerman, Franklin B. *Henry Purcell 1659-1695: His Life and Times.* New York: St. Martin's Press, 1967.

Historical and Theological Background

Boulger, James D. *The Calvinist Temper in English Poetry.* The Hague: Mouton Publishers, 1980.

Butterworth, Charles C. *The English primers, 1529-1545; their publication and connection with the English Bible and the Reformation in England.* Philadelphia: University of Pennsylvania Press, 1953.

Campbell, Lily B. *Divine Poetry and Drama in Sixteenth-Century England.* Cambridge: Cambridge University Press, 1959.

Clark, Ira. *Christ Revealed: The History of the Neotypological Lyric in the English Renaissance.* Gainesville: University of Florida Press, 1982.

Cunnar, Eugene Robert. 'Richard Crashaw and the Hymn Tradition: Seventeenth-Century Lord of the Lyre.' Ph.D. diss., University of Wisconsin, 1973.

Davies, Horton. *Worship and Theology in England from Andrews to Baxter and Fox, 1603-1690.* Princeton: Princeton University Press, 1975.

Dickens, A.G. *The English Reformation.* New York: Schocken Books, 1964.

Dyrness, William A. *Reformed Theology and Visual Culture: the Protestant Imagination from Calvin to Edwards.* Cambridge: Cambridge University Press, 2004.

Eistenstein, Elizabeth. *The Printing Press as an Agent of Change.* Cambridge: Cambridge University Press, 1979.

Evangelical Dictionary of Theology. Walter A. Elwell (ed.) Grand Rapids, MI: Baker Book House, 1984.

Galdon, Joseph A. *Typology and Seventeenth-Century Literature.* The Hague: Mouton & Co., 1975.

George, Charles H., and Katherine George. *The Protestant Mind of the English Reformation.* Princeton: Princeton University Press, 1961.

Grabo, Norman S. 'The Art of Puritan Devotion,' *Seventeenth-Century News* 26 (Spring, 1968): 7-9.

Hill, Christopher. *Society and Puritanism in Pre-Revolutionary England.* London: Seeker and Warburg, 1964.

_____ *A Tinker and a Poor Man: John Bunyan and His Church, 1628-1688.* New York: Alfred A. Knopf, 1989.

Huntley, Frank Livingstone. *Bishop Joseph Hall and Protestant Meditation in Seventeenth-Century England.* Binghamton, NY: Center for Medieval & Early Renaissance Studies, State University of New York at Binghamton,1981.

Kaufmann, U. Milo. *'The Pilgrim's Progress' and Traditions in Puritan Meditation.* New Haven: Yale University Press, 1966.

Keeble, N.H. *The Literary Culture of Nonconformity in Later Seventeenth- Century England.* Athens: University of Georgia Press, 1987.

King, John N. *English Reformation Literature: The Tudor Origins of the Protestant Tradition.* Princeton: Princeton University Press, 1982.

Knott, John R. *The Sword of the Spirit: Puritan Responses to the Bible.* Chicago: University of Chicago Press, 1980.

Ladell, A.R. *Richard Baxter, Puritan and Mystic.* London: Society for Promoting Christian Knowledge, 1925.

Lewalski, Barbara Kiefer. *Protestant Poetics and the Seventeenth-Century Religious Lyric.* Princeton: Princeton University Press, 1979.

Low, Anthony. *Love's Architecture: Devotional Modes in Seventeenth- Century English Poetry.* New York: New York University Press, 1978.

Martz, Louis L. *The Poetry of Meditation: a Study in English Religious Literature of the Seventeenth Century.* New Haven: Yale University Press, 1954

McDannell, Colleen, and Bernhard Lang. *Heaven: A History.* New Haven: Yale University Press, 1988

McGee, J. Sears. *The Godly Man in Stuart England: Anglicans, Puritans, and the Two Tables, 1620-1670.* New Haven: Yale University Press, 1976

Miller, Perry. *The New England Mind: The Seventeenth Century.* Cambridge: Harvard University Press, 1954.

Roston, Murray. *Biblical Drama in England.* Evanston: Northwestern University Press, 1965.

Schmidt, Leigh Eric. *Hearing Things: Religion, Illusion, and the American Enlightenment.* Cambridge: Harvard University Press, 2000.

Schucking, Levin L. *The Puritan Family: A Social Study from the Literary Sources.* Brian Battershaw (tr.) New York: Schocken Books, 1970.

Sommerville, C. John. 'On the Distribution of Religious and Occult Literature in Seventeenth-Century England.' *The Library* 29 (1974): 221-225.

_____ *Popular Religion in Restoration England.* Gainesville: University of Florida Press, 1977.

Stranks, C.J. *Anglican Devotion: Studies in the Spiritual Life of the Church of England between the Reformation and the Oxford Movement.* London: SCM Press Ltd., 1961.

Summers, David. *The Judgment of Sense: Renaissance Naturalism and the Rise of Aesthetics.* Cambridge: Cambridge University Press, 1987.

Vickers, Brian. *In Defence of Rhetoric.* Oxford: Clarendon Press, 1988.

Vinge, Louise. *The Five Senses: Studies in a Literary Tradition.* Lund, Sweden: LiberLaromedel Lund, 1975.

Wallace, Dewey D. (ed.) *The Spirituality of the Later English Puritans: an Anthology.* Macon, GA: Mercer University Press, 1987.

Wallace, Ronald S. *Calvin's Doctrine of the Word and Sacrament.* Tyler, Texas: Geneva Divinity School Press, 1953.

Webb, Stephen H. *The Divine Voice: Christian Proclamation and the Theology of Sound.* Grand Rapids, MI: Brazos Press, 2004.

White, Helen C. *English Devotional Literature 1600-1640.* Madison: University of Wisconsin Press, 1931.

_____ *The Tudor Books of Private Devotion.* Madison: University of Wisconsin Press, 1951.

Index